VOICES OF THE 21ST CENTURY

Bold, Brave, and Brilliant Women Who Make a Difference

GAIL WATSON

PUBLISHING

Published by
WSA Publishing
301 E 57th Street, 4th fl
New York, NY 10022

Manufactured in the United States of America, or in the United Kingdom when distributed elsewhere.

Watson, Gail
> *Voices of the 21st Century: Bold, Brave, and Brilliant Women*
> *Who Make a Difference*
> LCCN: 2019907847
> ISBN: 978-1-948181-62-4
> eBook: 978-1-948181-63-1

Cover design: Natasha Clawson
Copyediting: Claudia Volkman
Proofreading: Deb Coman
Interior design: Claudia Volkman

www.womenspeakersassociation.com

DEDICATION

We dedicate the stories in this book to you. May you find a connection within these pages and know that your message matters too. You, too, are a diamond who is here to Make a Difference.

CONTENTS

FOREWORD

Gail Watson

Our vision is of a world in which women
Are empowered to authentically express themselves;
To build a thriving, prosperous business;
And feel a part of something greater.
A world in which women take ownership of
And step into being the leaders that they are;
Using their voice to powerfully inspire others,
Thus causing transformation in the lives of their clients,
their companies, communities and the world.
—Women Speakers Association's Vision Statement

Since 2011, I have spoken to thousands of women from around the world, reaching into 120 countries. Each conversation has inspired, moved, and humbled me. I've learned so much and have been honored to hear their stories and how they've served. Women of different cultures, countries, ethnicities, religions, and backgrounds speaking their truth—person-to-person—in a conversation. A common thread woven through all their tales . . . a desire and need to share their voice and be heard.

In spite of the negative current narrative in the media and political arena that amplifies differences, now, more than ever, we are called to come together. Our truth is our sameness, our oneness, our stories.

I've handpicked these stories that were first shared in quiet conversation because each voice needs to be raised higher and wider to reach many, including you. I hope that you see yourself in some of the journeys and know that you are not alone. When we connect with each other, we focus on our similarities, our shared visions, and our hopes and dreams for a better future.

May each woman's personal journey leave you inspired and excited to make new connections. Listen with an open heart. Savor the triumphs and help carry the burdens. When we receive the story of another woman, we honor her and we honor ourselves.

I hope that each special message leaves you changed in some small way. May they bring to mind all the women in your life who need to hear them and need to share their own message. Reach out to them with love and listen to their story.

Like these, each story needs to be spoken, received, and recorded so that future generations can share in the knowledge that their story—their voice—matters. This is our legacy. Join me in embracing our brave women authors. They will forever be a Voice of the 21st Century.

"To the world you may be one person,
but to one person you may be the world." —Dr. Seuss

It is important for us to be reminded that our voice matters. How simple words when shared can change a person's day, year, or even their life—for better or for worse. Our ability to speak is perhaps our most powerful force as human beings, and how we choose to use our words makes all the difference in the world.

Each and every woman in this book has been gifted with a story—a story that lives within and through them to inspire you, the reader. Their motivation in sharing their truth is to teach you, guide you, and inspire you.

By sharing their stories, they hope to create more understanding that we are all unique, we all matter, and most importantly, we are all equal. They seek to stimulate your thinking, challenge the status quo, and bring light to once-dark topics. It has taken great courage for them to share their truth, to be open and vulnerable for the entire world to see. These women are trailblazers; they are bold, and they are brave. Their voices make a difference.

It is my privilege to introduce you to these amazing women, who range in age from twenty-one to sixty-plus. You will read about a young girl being branded a liar at age eleven, a woman who overcame the lifelong effects of no one believing she had been raped by a family member, and a woman's courageous struggle to break free of addiction. A failed suicide attempt was the best thing that ever happened to one of the authors. You'll read the heartbreaking story of a mother losing her nine-year-old son, and another's in-depth look into dementia. You'll meet the woman who's break from life was a few years in a tree house. You'll be inspired by the woman who tripled her business while battling breast cancer.

You'll meet young ladies in their twenties who will inspire you by their sense of leadership as they face struggles in today's climate. Plus so many more!

The diamond on our cover symbolizes that each author is proudly her unique self. Like a diamond, she is strong. She has been shaped differently— some flaws are bigger than others, some shine more brightly, and with her words in this book, her message is forever. Like the tip of the diamond, her message will also create ripple effects, one reader at a time.

There is no one right way or better way to express one's calling. One woman's message is not more significant because she has delivered it from the floor of the UN. There is no hierarchy when it comes to sharing our unique expression. So, remember . . . whether your stage is the classroom, the boardroom or the kitchen table—your voice matters!

In the pages that follow, I invite you to stay in your heart and, without judgment, receive each message being shared. Remember that behind each story is a woman bold and brave enough to have her voice be heard. This isn't about perfection or even about being in agreement; it's about honoring each of our distinct voices and the journey that brought us where we are today. By getting to know each one of these amazing women, you'll build new connections, and you'll realize that together we are building peace on earth.

Please support and encourage these women by sharing this book. If you feel a connection to a particular author's story, please reach out to her. She is here to serve you.

"She Is Bold, She Is Brave, She Is Brilliant, and She Is Making a Difference."

Gail Watson *is president and founder of Women Speakers Association (WSA),* **the** *go-to place for innovative leaders, change-agents, and women with a message to connect, collaborate, and grow their visibility worldwide in order to fulfill their mission. As the first-ever global community for women speakers, WSA provides a platform for women to get seen, booked, and paid AND be part of a growing network reaching women in 120 countries.*

www.womenspeakersassociation.com

Walking the Line
of Mental Health

Desiree Aragon

In 1956, newly married Johnny Cash wrote a song called "I Walk the Line." The song is considered his pledge of devotion to hold himself accountable to maintaining fidelity and avoiding rebel temptations in his relationship with his wife. It was Cash's first number-one hit. Those words *I walk the line* resonate deeply in my soul.

I'm forty-seven years old, and I feel as though I have spent my life walking the line. Trying to be everything everyone wants me to be—a good citizen, a good daughter, a good worker, a good wife, a good mother, a good human. Thanks to childhood experiences of molestation and domestic violence in my home, I grew up seeking safety. In his song Cash talks about keeping his eyes open at all times. That was me—hypervigilant, living in a state of heightened awareness, anticipating every possible scenario, and always hoping to prove my goodness and worth.

As a child I learned to do what was expected of me in order to stay safe. I was expected to be well behaved, not too visible, just present enough to be a good representative of the family. I brought this image into my adult working life and ultimately into my marriage. When my husband redirected my work choices, my life—previously filled with international travel—became very small.

To the outside world we looked like a typical American family: beautiful home, lakefront neighborhood, two cars, two dogs, two children, and a golf club membership. Even though we were outwardly living our dream, it was becoming more and more apparent that something needed shifting. My standard state of hypervigilant anxiety seemed to be evolving into a complacent sadness, a feeling of isolation. Simultaneously my husband's temper seemed to be increasing. He was angry about work, a broken heater system, and other things outside of our control. Our kids were facing challenges at school, so we were negotiating for counselors and accommodations.

Meanwhile, in my consultancy practice I was working with women to help them further develop their potential. I was guiding them to hold nothing back. In leading women to live bliss-filled lives, I began to take my own personal inventory. I was advising women on how to fully express themselves, yet something was missing in my own life. I started where I was, stepping back from my career goals to give my spouse extra one-on-one attention. He responded with even more anger. My effort to help us both find more fulfillment ultimately led to the demise of our relationship. I was looking to reignite our love, and instead the life we built came tumbling down. I was devasted. My feelings of isolation and despair grew even stronger.

To make matters more complicated, not only did our marriage fail, but the disruption in our children's lives—split households, new schools, and lost friends—resulted in difficulties all the way around. It was a mess. I felt like a hypocrite. How could I guide women to live their potential while everything around me was shattered? My marriage, my work, my home—everything was dismantled and filled with uncertainty. With this turn of events, my previously diagnosed generalized anxiety worked its way into a full-blown major depressive disorder.

The anxiety I had experienced since childhood reared up so strongly that I could no longer manage it. Believe me, I tried. Mindfulness, meditation, yoga, good nutrition, psychotherapy, supportive friendships, affirmations—I employed all my best skills, and still I was drowning in emotional turmoil. From the time of our marital separation in September 2017 up until April 2019, I could not have a conversation about my marriage, my children, or my work without it resulting in tears. I needed help in a way that went beyond all of the techniques I had learned up to that point.

In the fall of 2018, I had seen a psychiatrist and received the major depressive diagnosis, but in my stubbornness, I swore that I could get better using the homeopathic practices that had always worked for me in the past. I didn't want meds. I had gone forty-six years without them, so why would I take them now? Days, weeks, and months went by. I was barely getting out of bed, motivated only by the need to care for my children.

I finally reached the point where I had nothing left. Insignificant income, no savings, no self-esteem, and aside from my kids, nothing to live for. It was in this state of nothingness that I was finally willing to do something different. I contacted my local healthcare provider, was assigned a social worker, began seeing a psychiatrist, and enrolled in an intensive outpatient therapy program. I began taking antidepressants and began learning to rewire my brain to engage in life without hypervigilant anxiety.

Anticipating other people's responses to my actions has been core to my character since the early traumas I experienced in childhood. At some level I was afraid the antidepressants would turn me into a unfeeling monster. I had a secret fear that perhaps my true personality was cruel, selfish, and unkind. But what I am discovering is that the kindness in my heart is still very present. I am handling simple feedback easier, feeling less shame and guilt, and I can finally talk about my current state without crying.

I married for love, and my husband and I brought two beautiful children into the world and made a life together for fourteen years. When we divorced, I experienced incredible pain, and it woke me up to the truth of my mental state. I feel gratitude for the many homeopathic and traditional medical services that are helping me to find my way. I have finally let go of the need to prove my worth. I am learning to walk the line of my mental health without anxiety being the driving force of my existence. While tomorrow is filled with uncertainty, I have clearly turned a corner.

Desiree Aragon is a talent champion. She inspires women to discover what they do best and to maximize potential when it matters most. She is certified to train and facilitate top-rated leadership programs, and she assists her clients to deliver difficult messages and influence with the power of persuasion.

www.desireearagon.com

Pathway to Lasting Joy

Nasrin Barbic

"Your task is not to seek for love, but merely to seek and find all the barriers within yourself that you have built against it." —*Rumi*

So often when we are in a search for happiness, we look outside of ourselves. We search for the one who can make us happy, the perfect job, the perfect friends, and so on. People often think their experiences are coming at them from the outside in, but I've learned on my journey that our experiences come through us from the inside out.

In May 2013, I woke up—in a seemingly perfect life—feeling unhappy and confused. I had been married for ten years, had two wonderful boys, a successful career of thirteen years as a software engineer, lived in a beautiful house, and had no financial worries. And yet that morning I realized I was living a lie. I felt disconnected from myself, my husband, and even my children. I had done everything I was supposed to do. By all accounts I was successful, but I still didn't know who I was or what I really wanted. All I knew at that point was that I was not happy in my marriage or my job, and as much as I adored my boys, I wasn't showing up for them either because often I was lost in my thoughts. I felt as though I had been sleepwalking throughout my life.

Consequently, a year later I found myself in the middle of a divorce and feeling miserable. I could not stop the chatter in my head, which told me my husband and outside circumstances were to blame for the pain and sorrow I was experiencing. Looking back, I realized I had felt unloved and heartbroken before in my past relationships. The only difference this time was that I had kids, and I couldn't easily walk away as I had done in the past.

I started seeing a pattern in my life, and I became determined to figure out why I kept creating the same circumstances. My romantic relationships always started with a love affair but ended with me feeling disconnected and unloved. I decided to put my divorce on hold and focus on myself. My journey took me to yoga, meditation, life coaching, hypnotherapy, and energy healing, and what I learned in the process transformed my life.

Problem areas are a symptom of underlying hurts or limiting core beliefs; they are often unconscious but keep reasserting themselves in a variety of ways. Most of us carry emotional blockages. They can show up anywhere—in our relationships, at work, even in our body. These barriers can make us feel trapped in the same pattern over and over again, even when we're actively trying to change our lives. We often make choices and behave in ways that reinforce the very situations we don't want.

In my case, after going through hypnotherapy, I realized that because of my childhood circumstances and growing up among nine siblings, I felt invisible and unworthy of love. I had been totally unaware of this, but looking back I realized how I had sabotaged my relationships because I felt I was not enough, not lovable, and not worthy of attention.

Until we honestly come to terms with our limiting core beliefs and why we make the choices we make, change cannot occur. We often use our energy to try to change the people or situations in our lives, but this action renders us feeling depleted, frustrated, and angry. Our focus is in the wrong place—change is an inside job!

I had to learn to love myself. Practicing yoga allowed me to manage my stress and anxiety. Through meditation, I was able to quiet the negative chatter and replace it with more empowering thoughts. With the help of my coach, I learned to recognize the limiting beliefs that were holding me back from living an empowered life. I connected with my inner child through hypnotherapy, and I guided my inner child through the healing process. I learned that unless we heal our inner child, our true self will not be able to fully emerge.

In 2015, after two years of separation, my husband and I decided to get back together. In the end, it looked as though nothing had changed. I still had the same job, lived in the same house, was married to the same man—and yet everything was different because I was not the same person. One day, as I was playing with my nine-year-old son, he looked deep into my eyes and said, "Mom, I love the way you are now; please don't go back to the way you used to be." I used to be stressed, lost in my thoughts, short-tempered, angry, and anxious. Now I was at peace, content, joyful, present, and in love with life and myself.

Through finding myself, I also discovered my purpose and passion in life. I became a certified life coach, hypnotherapist, and Reiki master. I quit my full-time job as a software engineer and I now dedicate myself to helping others:

1. Create a clear vision for what they want out of life so they know where they're going and why they're going there.
2. Remove the frustrating blocks and limiting beliefs that are holding them back and replace them with positivity and possibility.
3. Become empowered to step into the life they long to live and manage relationships, work, and life with joy and ease.

I believe we create our lives from the inside out—we create our reality based on what we believe about ourselves and the world around us, consciously or unconsciously. Your inner thoughts, beliefs, and feelings create everything you see and experience in your outer world. The more you focus on changing your inner reality, the faster you will see new and amazing results in your outer reality! When you have nothing inside holding you back, there is nothing outside that can hold you back either.

Nasrin Barbic is a certified life coach, hypnotherapist, Reiki master, and founder of Pathway to Lasting Joy. Nasrin blends traditional coaching methods, scientifically proven techniques, and deep healing through hypnotherapy and Reiki to help clients release mental, physical, and spiritual blocks to success in all areas of their life.

www.pathwaytolastingjoy.com

LOVE SPOKEN HERE

Barbara Barry

Love spoken here: three simple words that I stitched onto an 8x10-inch preprinted needlepoint canvas. Little did I know that this Christmas gift to my parents in 1980 would become our informal family motto. Mom and Dad hung it near the back door, where most family and friends entered our home in Rhode Island.

For two decades, our family had lived far away from our relatives. With Dad in the Air Force, our parents' focus was on our family of seven. Over the years Mom typed and hand-wrote dozens of lengthy letters to her family and Dad's. We visited our grandparents, alternating between sets, every year until we moved to Germany. Mom and Dad made friends easily and welcomed company, immersing us quickly in our new communities. Living and traveling in Europe, Mom frequently commented, "Even though we're different, we're all the same."

Settling near Grandma Skurka and many family members, we savored the joy of seeing them frequently. Along with our relatives came a steady stream of our friends, some of whom our family unofficially adopted. As we kids grew up and moved elsewhere, we always loved coming home. We brought with us our broken hearts and dreams, our pets, our beloved spouses, and our own beloved children. We were always welcome, no matter the reason for our visit, no matter the "baggage" we carried. Mom and Dad loved us through it all, whether in sorrow or joy.

One winter changed everything. Oh, Mom and Dad continued to love us all, but now it was our turn to serve them. Dad had a major stroke, losing his mobility and speech. Mom's health declined precipitously. Each of my siblings contributed to Mom and Dad's care, whether by medical advocacy, financial expertise, or loving visits. Ten months after Dad's stroke, Mom died with Dad at her side. It was the year from hell.

Despite his right-sided paralysis, inability to speak, and losing the love of his life, Dad humbly carried his cross. He became a shining light of love. He fully understood what we said and what was happening around him. Observing a fellow patient or a staff member having a bad day, he wheeled over and patted their hand. He greeted everyone's visitors with a lefty handshake and a big smile. When we knelt next to his chair or bed, he hugged us with his left arm and all his beautiful love. Although Dad had no realistic hope of recovering his full health, still he ministered to those around him. How he inspired hope for our own lives!

Years later, love made me do the hardest thing I had ever done up to that time: I called the police to arrest my son Michael. Since adolescence he had struggled continually with mental illness and depression. A couple months after a hospitalization for suicidal tendencies, he began acting strangely and answered angrily when I questioned him. Going outside, I first called my husband and then 911. Meanwhile, John called Mike. After listening to Mike's furious tirade, John told him, "There's nothing you can do that can make me stop loving you." Mike calmed down immediately. What had changed? Only Mike's understanding that, even in that explosive moment, his dad loved him thoroughly and unconditionally. At the request of Mike's therapist, the judge turned Mike over to our custody that afternoon, stipulating that he be admitted immediately to Butler Hospital for severe depression and anxiety. Though his depression was unknown to most people, his ongoing treatment and our love helped Mike continue living with his illness.

Five years later, leaving us a beautiful note expressing his love, Mike prepared us as well as he could for the worst day of our lives, when we lost him.

John's words describe our world seven years later.

Emerging from our son's long and valiant battle with mental illness, depression, and subsequent suicide, we have made a startling discovery: we can endure anything. Though we still miss him profoundly—and always want to—we have rediscovered joy. And the glory of wonder. And the thrill of possibilities. We thought we'd never experience those things again. Thank God—literally.

But wait—although we still experience deep grief for days or weeks, how can we be even somewhat at peace without Mike physically present in our lives? Much of our peace comes from knowing that we loved him as thoroughly as we could, and that he loved us thoroughly too. Still more comes from the continued loving support of family members, friends, and even strangers with whom we have shared Mike's story. Much peace we attribute to faith: ours, Mike's, and that of all the people who pray for us. We have faith that we will see Mike again after this life.

Finally, our peace springs from the inspiration of Rwanda. Sixteen years after the genocide that massacred nearly a million people in three months, our daughter volunteered there as a teacher-translator in a Catholic school. When one of her students pointed to a nearby cemetery and said, "That's where my mother is buried," Laura struggled to reconcile the horror and heartbreak that had occurred with the comparative peace now. The answer lay in forgiveness and unity. When John and I visited her there, the parish priests confirmed that the family members of the victims had genuinely forgiven the killers. Forgiveness helped the survivors to heal.

The other remarkable characteristic of Rwanda's evolution is unity. The genocide was one major tribe's attempt to eliminate the other. The new government prohibited the use of tribal references, in order to foster unity. The love of the Rwandan people showed our family a preview of heaven on earth. "We are Rwandans." Their expression is *Turi Kumwe* ("We Are Together"). We are one, united by love with every human being.

Whether we are separated from loved ones by death, distance, or damaged relationships, let's remember that "we are together."

Choose love.

Make peace.

Embrace as your personal motto "Love spoken here"!

Barbara Barry is a technology problem solver, speaker, and connector of people. She empowers adults to understand, enjoy, and use their computers, tablets, and smartphones, especially to communicate with loved ones. Happily married for thirty-six years, Barb and her husband have two grown children, one in Washington, D.C., and one in heaven.

www.barrybasic.com

STILL IN THE GAME

Melody Breyer-Grell

"Hey," I cried out to a young student and recent acquaintance, "could I have one of your sausages?"

Without waiting for his response, I swiped a patty off his plate and scarfed it down quickly, as if the inappropriate, intimate action would prevent the burning pain I inevitably experienced in my stomach.

My classmates were used to my occasionally eccentric behavior. Six months earlier, breaking in a new pair of shoes during my previous graduate residency (I was taking my post-menopausal MFA in Creative Writing), I tripped on the sidewalk, landing face down on the pavement and breaking my nose. Donning dark shades, I made it to class the next morning, though there had been enough blood on the pavement to spark rumors of a wild shoot-out. I quickly became a legend.

Upon my return to school six month later, my wheezing lungs, dependence on Depends (suddenly having lost urinary continence), and inability to ingest a meal did not cause my colleagues much concern. Perhaps they thought it was due to my pharma-cocktail. Nor did my puffy body, pale skin, and slurred speech surprise anyone. I was merely a big, hot mess.

Despite my infirmities, I vowed to present my "scholarly" paper. Ostensibly unconcerned about my delivery, this was merely bravado that masked the insecurity shared by many "creatives." Merely existing in survival mode, my ego flew away, disintegrating into the frozen Western Pennsylvanian air. I just needed to make it through. To abandon, at my age, yet another endeavor, would brand me as a feckless dilettante.

The reading was held in the school's historical mansion, the home of the university's original founders. Ironically scheduled last to read, I took my place before the crowd and groped the podium. A long, billowing scarf served as my security blanket, and as if it were by magic, my voice strengthened. In a flash I realized that for once I truly didn't care what the group thought of me—the controversial nature of my thesis buoyed me on. The embarrassment I had originally experienced when manically choosing my topic—"Obscenity and Humor in Memoir"—melted away as I enjoyed the sincere recognition of my colleagues.

The reality was that, although the residency had just begun with our readings, for me, with my failing body, it was finished. Although I doggedly followed my millennial buddy Angie across the elegant hallway to the day's final event, I sat through it knowing I would not see another classroom anytime soon.

I quickly deflated akin to a Macy's balloon—ready to pack it in—possibly to return for next year's parade. All hopes of revisiting my youth with Angie and the new kids evaporated.

That night the class and staff assembled in the hotel bar. I won't say the student body was encouraged to drink, as we were NOT, *but* as we were writers, there was no dissuasion of such activity. Always more interested in chocolate and Klonopin than drink, the bar was not my natural habitat, but it certainly was everyone else's. I was wearing my heaviest sweater and my winter faux-down, full length coat with the aforementioned scarf tied around my neck. I found my mentor standing by the bar, his eyes welcoming as I sidled by his coterie. Although weak, I was almost floating—maybe it was the lack of oxygen to my brain, for the white light seemed to be charging up in the heavens.

"I am out of here, Jack. Sorry, I am toast. I can't breathe or eat . . ."

I felt the love of my teacher, a handful of my colleagues, and my equivalent sentiment toward them, minus the often desperate narcissism which haunted much of my life. There was life beyond my reckless individualism, and I could have both friendship and a creative existence.

Swept home by my overly attentive husband, I attempted to heal on my own, but following two sips of some old-fashioned, savory chicken soup, my lungs burned and closed up, rendering me momentarily terrified. I screamed and choked the very few blocks toward the hospital, hoping my husband would not find me completely histrionic. He grabbed a cab to make it the last hundred yards to the emergency room, as I was almost finished.

The young doctor reported the results of a couple of scans and then made her pronouncement.

"I have good news and bad news," she began. "Your lungs don't seem to have an embolism, but your abdomen, your pelvic area, has a very large mass."

"Benign?" I said, knowing the answer was not that. My fear, the premonition of the big C, came to pass. Cancer. I was tentatively diagnosed with stage four ovarian cancer, a condition that's almost impossible to diagnose in an early stage. In my case it tricked me into believing that I was suffering from other organic difficulties. Instead, the hungry tumors feeding off my body's resources were the cause of all my respiratory and digestive dysfunction. Dreading any type of treatment, I asked the doctor if I could just take painkillers and fade away. Shocked by my request, she warned that if I did not shrink the tumors with chemo, my passing would be anything but peaceful, as I would drown in the liquid that caused my recent distress.

So much for becoming resigned to my disease. Following genetic testing, I was found to carry BRCA — a genetic flaw that appears mostly (but not exclusively) in the Ashkenasi Jewish population, affecting both men and women.

While I'm still in an early stage of treatment, I seem to be improving, thanks to the extensive research geared toward BRCA. I'm committed to spreading the word about BRCA to anyone. Once again, I have found something else to make noise about, and I will continue to do so, hoping to serve others as I continue to orate, true to my inborn vocation.

Melody Breyer-Grell made her professional writing debut by penning the lyrics to her satirical cabaret show, What's So Funny About Jazz? *She has written for* Cabaret Scenes Magazine, Bass Musician Magazine, *and* Hot House Jazz. *A frequent contributor to the* Huffington Post Arts and Entertainment *section, she broadly opines on a large range of subjects.*

https://www.facebook.com/melody.grell

My Life, My Terms

Natasha Clawson

My corporate job came to an abrupt, screaming halt in January 2019.

I'd been with this particular company for roughly four years, during which I'd rapidly climbed the ladder from executive admin all the way to a director-level position.

As the company grew and changed, I found that although I was in alignment with their purpose-driven mission, other values that mattered deeply to me had become incongruent. Try as I might, I no longer fit within the organization.

However, I couldn't seem to move forward. Should I go back into business for myself (I had been a freelance designer), or should I find another corporate position? In my heart, I knew I wanted to pursue entrepreneurship . . . but I was afraid. When I had worked for myself previously, I had hustled so hard that I eventually burned myself out. I had experienced massive anxiety resulting from improper boundaries and a lack of experience and resources.

At this point, I felt recharged and equipped to leave, but that self-doubt lingered. I continued to waffle on the decision, all the while becoming more and more miserable at work. Eventually I had a very open conversation with leadership about the lack of alignment I felt, and what had led up to this divide. This resulted in my abrupt termination.

Years ago, this conversation would have been devastating, earth-shattering, and insurmountable. In fact, it never would have happened. I was raised to *never* give any indication of being unhappy at a job. If you were leaving, you didn't tell them until you had another job and your two-weeks' notice in hand.

But in the four years that I had been with this company, I had learned a lot about honest conversations, and I'm not someone who holds back—even at the cost of a job. I also learned that turnover doesn't have to be a bad thing. I had seen countless people leave a position they didn't love and go on to do wonderful things somewhere else!

So many people (myself included) get overly attached to a job. It is easy to become so invested in the identity you build there, or the dependence on a paycheck—or even your family or spouse's expectations of who and what you should be—that you lose sight of what's *right* for you.

I know I delayed leaving because I was worried about the expectations of my friends and family, especially the opinion of my fiancé. Our financial obligations didn't make this any easier. We had just bought our first house (in California, no less!) and were still in full-throttle saving mode for our fast-approaching wedding.

Despite my concerns, my family and fiancé were more supportive than I could have envisioned. The timing was perfect, and leaving my corporate job opened up doors for me that had been inaccessible before. My creativity blossomed, and I felt the weight of exhaustion that I had been carrying around lift. When I felt that lightness, I knew I was back on my path. I could be nothing but thankful for the circumstances that had led me to this point.

I still wish I had had the courage and trust in myself to leave my corporate job when I realized there was no future there. It would have saved me months of pain.

Maybe if we weren't so afraid of the stigma of leaving a job or being let go, we'd have more honest conversations sooner and help people who aren't in the right place get to the *right* destination faster, instead of spending months or years *trapped* in a job they dislike.

A Gallup poll reported that 70 percent of people in the United States aren't engaged in their jobs.[1] That's insane! Especially since these people are waking up every day and *choosing* to go to this job. We're not indentured servants—but sometimes we act like it.

If you're where I was, I've got news for you: you don't have to wait! You're in control of your life and your choices.

No matter what other people think, this is *your* life. And if you aren't happy somewhere, then it's time to evaluate what's going on and fix it or make a change. Only *you* have that power in your life. **No one else is going to do it for you.**

Let's quit being so damn afraid. Let's be open to changing as many times and as often as we need to. The path of life is not linear—it's a journey of constant growth, enlightenment, and discovery.

And just so we're clear, I'm not saying that everyone should be an entrepreneur. Sometimes I wonder if it's right for me!

And that's OK. You should constantly be evaluating, changing, and evolving. What was right yesterday may not be right today. If you stop holding on to what you think you must be, and instead be willing to flow with what is true for yourself, you will experience a higher level of fulfillment.

This approach to life is starting a new wave in business. Together, we're creating the modern workplace where work and life are no longer separate, but integral.

We are building a supportive and encouraging workplace and world where *every single one of us beautiful, magical human beings* can feel loved and accepted. We all have a perfect fit and we need to help each other discover it.

Whether it's telling yourself to move on, or helping someone else along their path, let this story serve as your inspiration. Wherever you are, be there intentionally. Don't get stuck somewhere because of your expectations of how things "should" be.

You only have this one life, so *live* it on your terms.

---

[1] https://news.gallup.com/opinion/chairman/212045/world-broken-workplace.aspx?g_source=position1&g_medium=related&g_campaign=tiles.

Natasha Clawson is a graphic designer and brand enthusiast. She helps businesses create visual brand identities with a sense of clarity and composure that positions them for growth. She's a proud millennial and tireless champion of healthy workplace culture and mental health.

www.aspireenco.com

CORE PURPOSE: THE TINIEST MATRYOSHKA DOLL

Deb Coman

To see her today, you would be hard-pressed to envision the carefree, lighthearted, chatty person she always was. Unless, of course, you could see beyond the physical challenges the years saved up and bombarded her with all at once. If you (as my sisters and dad and I) had connected with the essence of her before now, you'd close your eyes and bring back her vibrant personality to this silent body in a nursing home. It's what we do. It's the only thing we can do.

What is it that makes us who we are even when our bodies betray us? What is our essence underneath the surface? How do we get there and preserve it?

Beyond her body, even beyond her quiet eyes, she is still there. She is still Mom. The essence of her is in there, somewhere. And for now, it has to be enough. Our souls know each other, even without conversation. We all remain connected.

But what is this essence that makes her "her"? Clearly not the body that doesn't work the way it did all the years before. And not the voice, now unheard most days. Her heart remains strong in spite of its partner parts and systems no longer doing their jobs. Her spirit remains. The connection to that is strong. Her inner strength and will are palpable, even on the darkest of days.

Our essence is more than how our bodies show up. It is more than our voice; it's more than how we engage in the world. It often lives beyond the grasp of our language. Though we feel it in our hearts and minds, we fumble to describe it in words. When we name it, our reward is the connection that it brings . . . the connection beyond our physical presence.

Stripping away the layers to reveal our own core doesn't come naturally.

There's a tug of war between wanting to know what's in there and not wanting everyone else to see. It takes time and help to entice it into the light. We must feel safe and still be brave.

The words we'll eventually choose to talk about our essence do matter. The nuances of their meaning are important. In my strategy work with business owners to hone their messaging and content, defining their core message and values is step one. Uncovering the core is slippery and elusive at first. It requires excavation and a willingness to go deep.

Why we do what we do and who we really are—our core purpose—is central to everything that follows. It's impossible and unwise to build a house on a flimsy foundation. As business owners, speakers, authors . . . as people . . . all our language comes from this. When we define ourselves and our work through a website, an email, an article, or a talk, it comes from our core message.

If you haven't identified this core in language that captures it clearly, your foundation is not solid. Alignment in your message is critical to establish trust. It's essential for consistent connection with the people you intend to reach. It's the thread that ties all of what you do and who you are together. It's a language that speaks beyond the body.

Exploring core messaging for business owners is an honor that fills my soul with joy and my eyes with tears at times. Using a process that fosters safety, connection, and ease, I'm in awe of what's uncovered each time I do this. Helping someone to see her or his own essence, often in a new light and with new language, is truly a privilege.

Uncovering core messaging involves repeatedly asking why as we go deeper into the layers and label what emerges. The process is similar to a matryoshka—a Russian nesting, or babushka, doll where each wooden doll has another smaller one within it. As we shed the outer layers, we eventually arrive at a small, yet mighty core . . . the tiniest matryoshka doll. She defines our core essence.

In my own un-nesting of the dolls, I began with the largest matryoshka: I helped business owners write and edit their messaging. Why? Because clear messaging is critical to effective communication. But there was a smaller matryoshka within: to create messages that attract and compel the right people to buy. Why? Because clear messaging has intention. And then, a smaller matryoshka still: strategy in messaging to share and repurpose it. Why? Because intention needs a specific action plan. And still then, the tiniest matryoshka: to create meaningful connection between you and your customers. Again, why? Because people buy from people, and *you* are the essence of your business. It is only through communicating your true, real core that you can stand out in a sea of online noise.

Your why is my why. I desperately want your message to reach the people you're meant to serve. I want your business and your life to thrive. When you do, I do too. And my teeny, tiniest matryoshka is to live the life that fills my heart with joy and inspires me, one that gives me time, prosperity, and meaningful experiences with my family.

The tiniest matryoshka that lives inside my mom still shows. I witness her strength. She has endured physical discomfort and body function betrayal more painful and long-lasting than many of us ever will. In spite of it all, her will to live, her spirit, and her inspiration is stronger than all her challenges combined. I see you, tiniest matryoshka. I see you.

May you have a person and a process to excavate your core essence and communicate it with the world. It will strengthen you in your purpose and become a beacon that attracts the right people you're meant to serve. Without one, you are untethered. Once revealed, your tiniest matryoshka will bring you clarity, connection, and all the success you can imagine. It would be my honor to share your journey.

Deb Coman is a content conversion strategist, copywriter, and speaker. Her copy is behind some of the big-name Facebook™ ads you see, and her strategies power many blogs, social media sites, and email campaigns. By aligning with core values, Deb supports business owners to attract and convert through connection.

www.DebComan.com

IT'S NEVER TOO LATE TO LIVE
A LIFE YOU LOVE

Janine JJ Conway

I still wake up some mornings, look across the bed, and say to myself in disbelief, "This amazing man can't possibly be *my* husband." It has to be a dream. Someone else's good dream—one I'm not good enough to have. Not after the nightmare I lived for over thirty years. The nightmare feels more right, more comfortable, more *normal.* Those mornings are rarer and rarer, but they still come.

It's hard to describe my upbringing in a balanced way. Although I know there were some good times (Mom has pictures to prove it), abuse is woven through my memories until my mom left my dad when I was thirteen. Though Mom reared us to be independent, my psyche was already programmed to accept emotional and physical abuse as normal.

I had two boyfriends in college: the first went to jail for assault, and the other I dated for three years. I ended the relationship when he became too controlling, but I then yielded to family pressure to marry him anyway. "After all," one of my close female family members said, "no one else is barking up your tree, and you don't want to end up old and alone." In her day, if you weren't engaged by the time you graduated from college, your chances of marrying were abysmal.

Our marriage quickly deteriorated into controlling and abusive behavior. After four years I tried to leave, but certain forms of spousal abuse, including rape, were legal in some states back then. Even in states that criminalized sexual and physical abuse against a spouse, those laws were rarely enforced. If I left, it would be without a "divorce without cause," which, due to the very-high security clearance I held, would be grounds for losing my job.

The biggest hurdle, though, was my faulty beliefs. If I would just stop being so selfish and needy and be a good enough wife, I thought, he'd go back to being my best friend, not this monster in front of me. I foolishly thought I could "love" him back to his old self. I knew my best friend was in there somewhere: I saw him behind the pulpit every Sunday as he preached.

The one bright light from that relationship is my first son. It took eight years and several losses to finally be able to hold this miracle baby in my arms. He is what eventually motivated me to stop tolerating the abuse. After all, the way he saw his father treat me would be the way he'd grow up to treat me (and other women).

My husband resigned from his position, and to make ends meet, I volunteered for a six-month military trip. It was the first time I felt the Spirit leading me to do something contrary to my understanding of Scripture (since "Man is head of the household"). I also felt led to open a separate bank account for the trip, and I remember the day I did, fingers trembling over the mouse because I was doing something that contradicted God's decree that wives should "submit to their husbands," yet I felt strongly I should do it.

I now know God is a kind and loving Father who cares for His children. He was leading me just as any earthly father would if he knew what his baby girl was going through!

I came home from that trip to find my house sold and most of my belongings thrown out. We signed divorce papers five days later. He went off looking young enough with his wavy hair to attract college girls. I went off to learn how to be a broke single military mom, with over $845,000 of divorce debt.

On one hand, life was tough, and I used a lot of cardboard boxes for furniture. But on the other hand, I was free from fifteen years of abuse I had tried to hide "for the sake of my husband's ministry."

When I finally started dating again, I seemed to only attract predators! I still felt unworthy of nice things, nice people, and nice experiences, but it was a huge step forward that I could at least recognize that these men would tear down all I had built up financially and professionally. This was another step forward: valuing myself enough to protect myself.

Eventually, and I'm still not sure how it happened, I began to attract more abundance into my life: abundant finances, abundant friendships, and abundant fruit in both community work and a ministry I started.

There's a saying, "The sexiest thing a woman can put on is confidence," and I started attracting higher-caliber men. Unfortunately, I couldn't get past my past. When a man's mannerisms (in any way) were reminiscent of my dad or ex-husband, I dropped him! I was never going to need a man again. Want? Sure. Need? Never!

One man broke through my defenses and built a friendship—a partnership—with me. We called or Skyped each other every night for almost three years until we married.

This man carried me through deployments in the Middle East, debilitating car accidents, and the roller coaster of starting my own business. His strengths make up for my many weaknesses, and he meets most of my emotional needs just by being himself.

I am passionate about working in a singles ministry now, often reminding my singles that "it's better to be alone than to be miserably married and better to be single and alone than to be married and alone." I encourage them to be faithful to themselves while they wait, and I support those who choose to remain single.

When I look at the pain and sorrow of the first part of my life, I realize that the last amazing eight years have been worth every tear I've shed. It's never too late to start over. It's never too late to begin to love yourself. It's never too late to have the experiences you dream of. It's never too late—as long as you're willing to take the first step. And that first step is making the decision *today* to take ownership of your own life!

Janine "JJ" Conway returned from a six-month military trip to discover her house sold, her stuff thrown out, and $845,000 in divorce debt to her name. JJ turned creativity into a thriving business and now helps others succeed using the same personal growth and financial management skills that worked for her.

www.JJConway.org

YOU NEVER KNOW WHO IS WATCHING YOU

Tami Damian

"You made it! I knew you'd make it," the sweet little girl's voice called out. I looked up to see her large smile as she skipped toward me. I wasn't sure who she was talking to, and then I realized it was me. I had just rounded the last bend up the Bright Angel Trail at the South Rim of the Grand Canyon, and yes, I had made it to the top.

I heard her mother's voice saying, "Can we get lunch now?" Then her father rounded the bend and told me, "She's been watching you for hours and would not leave for lunch until she knew you made it up here."

Tears burned my eyes, blending with my sweat and the rain. She wasn't the only one wondering if I'd make it. That morning my husband asked more than once if I'd be OK hiking alone. He was headed to the North Rim, and I was heading back up to the South Rim. It was a mere four and a half miles from the Indian Garden Campground to the top of the South Rim. I had prepared and planned; I was ready. But I still questioned myself—would I really make it on my own? I was physically tired. I had an injured knee, and I was emotionally exhausted and spiritually weary. I had recently lost my mother after six months of watching her health go up and down and then down and down; I never got to say good-bye to her.

This little girl's dad told me they had talked about some of the explorers of the Grand Canyon, and at some point his daughter asked why all of the stories were about men. Her momma told her women didn't hike. The little girl told her momma that she would hike the canyon one day so there would be stories about girls too.

Her dad continued telling me that his daughter spotted me far below from the Visitor's Center via the pay-per-view binoculars. I was, in fact, wearing a bright green bandana and a hot pink shirt. Perhaps I chose that colored clothing in case I slipped—in case I fell. People fall into the canyon often, and I wouldn't have minded not hurting anymore. I missed my mom. I felt very alone. My body hurt; my heart hurt. A misstep would have been easy. My eyes kept brimming with tears as I looked at this beautiful little creature watching me in awe.

The little girl told me she had spotted me standing alone on the trail and was so excited about seeing a girl hiking that she kept watching me. She said she didn't want me to reach the top alone, so she decided she'd watch me and make sure I made it. She told me she even passed up ice cream so she could keep an eye on me. Her father laughed and said ice cream would have been cheaper than the quarters he kept feeding into the viewfinder.

There was a time during the hike when I was completely alone on the trail. At that point I was done. I screamed out, "Is anyone out there?" I fell to my knees and screamed up at the sky, "You? Are you even out there?" Nothing. I knew it. Yet I couldn't take that step off the trail. It just didn't seem fair to those still living and loving me. And I kept hearing this voice saying, "Get up and move forward. Get up and move forward . . ."

With several feet of trail still to go, I struggled to talk between my tears and trying to breathe. "So, you want to be a Grand Canyon hiker, eh?" I asked her.

"Yes ma'am," she told me eagerly.

I got down on my knee and told her, "Honey, you can do anything you want, if you just set your heart on it, set goals, prepare, and then start."

Wow! Those were exactly the words my mother had told me over and over in my life. She believed in me like no one else. And yes, I had made it.

"I'm ready to start," the little girl exclaimed. "But I have a question for you. Why are you mad at God?"

Oh my, she must have seen me yell. Thank God she did not see me step off the edge. "I'm kind of mad at the world right now," I told her honestly.

The little girl told me that when she saw that I was yelling at God, she got on her knees and prayed for me. "I figured I was closer to Him than you were anyway," she said. She told me her prayer was simple: "Get up and move forward."

What? That message has been my company tag line since 2002. *She must be an angel!*

She asked if she could hold my hand for the last steps. I handed her one of my hiking poles and took her hand. I realized then that I had never been alone on that hike. I had my husband hiking the other way, my mother was overseeing my steps, and my new friend was waiting for me at the top.

Once we reached the Rim, her dad took our picture and then took one of me alone with my camera. His daughter was so excited; she told me she had never had her picture taken with a hero before. A hero? I am just a middle-aged, overweight woman from Nebraska that made what many would consider a small hike up a common trail. I told her she could be a hero, too, if she followed her heart and did what made her happy. She told me she wanted to be the first black girl to hike the Grand Canyon, and I decided it was up to her dad to tell her that girls (and women) of all colors have hiked this canyon. Then the girl and her family agreed it was lunchtime, and just as quickly as they had appeared, the family was gone

It comforts me to know that somewhere that little girl has a photo of us and the understanding that girls and women can do anything they want, including hike the Grand Canyon. I hope she realizes her dream. And I need to remember the lesson that someone is always watching me. I had made it—but not by myself. You never know who's watching you. Is your behavior worthy of being someone's hero? Life gives us the lessons, it's up to us to learn them.

*Storyteller, teacher, trainer, author, advocate, friend, sister, aunt, wife, and daughter all describe **Tami Damian**, president of Leadership Education And Development, Inc. Tami's passion is helping others find their passion and purpose. She is a Zig Ziglar Legacy Certified Trainer and Coach, a speaker, and the author of the* Life Lessons Learned *series.*

www.LEADGroup.net

FIRE UP YOUR DREAM MACHINE
—LET'S GET TO WORK!

Kiley Doll

I grew up in a chaotic military family with ten brothers and sisters. We were a mix of biological siblings and foster kids—a whirlwind family moving from place to place. It wasn't the easiest lifestyle, and I know it was a bit of a struggle for my "tribe," but I loved it! Moving around so much gave me the chance to reinvent myself each time I changed schools. How many kids have the chance to really embrace that kind of opportunity?

My father was a tough, self-made, self-taught man with a serious drive for business and life. After retiring from the Air Force, my father started a construction business. As "Daddy's Little Girl," I worked with him whenever I had the chance. When I was nine years old, he was remodeling a strip center and I told him, "When I grow up, I want to own one of these."

When he asked me why, my answer was pretty much a foreshadowing of what was to come: "So I can put all of my business in each of the stores."

My passion for business came from my father, but my entrepreneurial resilience and training came from the School of Hard Knocks. My life took a serious turn at the age of sixteen, when I faced motherhood a lot earlier than most. It might not have been the ideal turn of events, but sometimes blessings come in truly unexpected disguises. God gave me babies early because he knew I wouldn't sit still long enough later. Life as a teenage mom definitely wasn't easy. More than once I found myself wondering which direction was up. But I rallied for the sake of my beautiful children as well as myself and climbed my way back up again.

I could have been content where I was. But I'm not really a simple "lemons-into-lemonade"-type of woman. I want all the fruit and then some! If there was one principle I learned, it was "how to clean up after my own messes." I was a ferocious self-learner. I read and studied everything I could to better myself.

I spent the next twenty years building and running more than five businesses, including a yogurt shop, a resale store, a Cajun restaurant and bar, and I headed up a successful real estate team too. Some of my businesses excelled. Some of them flopped. But not for one second did I give up. I kept my loved ones on their toes with whatever I decided to do next. I taught my kids by example that if you don't love what you do, change it.

Today I'm proud of the path that has led me to become the co-founder of a MarTech company, a successful real estate investor, and an avid mentor and business coach. It's been a long road, full of twists and turns, and that's exactly the way I like it! I took the road less traveled—several roads, actually—and now I find myself in a place where I can uplift and inspire. There isn't a person who can't be mentored if they are willing to do the work; I'm proof positive of that.

A common complaint among entrepreneurs is that they spend less time with their families during those first few crucial years of building a business. My experience was entirely different. I'm lucky to have such a supportive family—they truly share my passion and believe that I'm a superwoman.

On average, I work ten to twelve-hour days, a feat that would be daunting for most people. Luckily for me, I'm a high energy person. I play as hard as I work. This schedule is my ideal, but it definitely isn't for everybody. You've got to find your own groove. That's where the magic happens.

All entrepreneurs make sacrifices; it's part of the ball game. You need to know exactly what price you're willing to pay to get ahead. Don't ever do something that doesn't feel right—that's a slippery slope to regret. Do what you want to do and find the best possible way to do it.

It's never too late to make a change or start something new. Remember that.

What were your dreams, aspirations, business concepts, or things you thought about but didn't DO anything about? If you don't have any of your own ideas right now, borrow some from your friends— they didn't use 'em!

Ask yourself some simple questions:

- What do your friends say you are good at?
- What are your natural talents?
- What would you love to do if money was no object?

Grab hold of any ideas you generate during this self-reflective process and start scribbling. Don't second-guess yourself. Just jot down whatever pops into your head. You can sort it all out later.

- Which of your ideas make you smile?
- Which ones work within your current lifestyle?
- Which ones need a little more wiggle room?

Google the ideas you've generated. This process is more eye-opening than you might think. What you're doing right now is some personal A/B testing. You're giving yourself a chance to learn where the income possibilities might be—and it doesn't take much more than some soul-searching to figure it out.

You don't need a business plan to start a business or change a career. You need a vision and passion; this can't be taught. I have been known to say I can't want something more than you; I don't know how to turn the lights off. Now go out and fire up your dream machine—you have work to do.

Kiley Doll was born to be an entrepreneur— it's in her bones. She is an experienced business development professional and real estate investor. As a sought-after coach, she combines her zest for life and drive for business with her passion for empowering struggling entrepreneurs. She's never met a person she can't help.

www.kileyco.biz

How Your Story Can Turn into a Movement

Tracey Ehman

When I was invited to share my story in the first *Voices of the 21st Century* collaborative book, I wasn't sure what I wanted to share. I generally don't like drawing attention to myself, preferring to be supportive of others and blending into the crowd . . . being seen but not heard and trying not to ruffle any feathers. But when I was diagnosed with breast cancer at the age of forty-two, something changed. Like many things in my life, however, it took a while for that change to become apparent.

It is unfathomable the kind of impact you can have when you are willing to be vulnerable and share your story with people who are close to you as well as those you have never met.

I found sharing my story so cathartic. It allowed me to put my thoughts into words—and seeing those words in print made me feel a peace I never knew I was looking for. It gave me confidence that my story was being received by those who needed to hear the lessons I'd learned. Having the right mindset and building my business helped keep me sane during my treatments, much less likely to dwell on the "what ifs" and instead focusing on the "what can be."

Because of that, I felt compelled to begin a new project called The Silver Lining of Cancer. I had actually purchased the domain name five years before, knowing that at some point in my life, I wanted to share my story in some format as a way to help others.

As a result of being involved with *Voices of the 21st Century*, I knew that the first step was a collection of cancer stories called *The Silver Lining of Cancer*, with the common thread being each author's ability to find the silver lining, even in dire circumstances. So many people are diagnosed daily, and the negative thoughts can far outweigh the positive. This collaborative book was not only created as a vehicle for those who had experienced a cancer diagnosis for themselves or family member, but also to spread positivity, hope, and love around the world. It has become my mission to reach out to women who want to share their inspirational stories in the hopes of making a difference—no matter how small—in the lives of others who were walking a similar journey.

When you or your family faces a life-threatening or life-changing diagnosis of cancer (or any disease), many thoughts will crowd your mind. Some of the thoughts that came to me were:

> "Am I still going to be here to see my kids graduate, start careers, build their families?"

> "Why me? I've never hurt anyone, why am I being afflicted with this disease?"

> "No good deed goes unpunished!" (This was my go-to at one point when I was feeling especially bitter.)

Any and all of these are normal responses and are OK. We each deal with news and circumstances differently, and we need to let these thoughts surface, and then get them out of our system.

When I began sharing my vision, I didn't think of The Silver Lining of Cancer as a movement until I started to hear people calling it a movement in conversations with others and on interviews. It seemed that by taking a chance and sharing my message, my vision, and my hopes, people were responding in a very positive way.

My vision is to provide hope and inspiration to people touched by cancer across the globe.

I have experienced waiting for appointments, being hooked up to chemo, feelings of despair about the changes in my body, and the devastation of losing my hair. Picking up a *People* magazine in the waiting room just didn't cut it. Instead I believe that reading stories of inspiration, such as the ones featured in *The Silver Lining of Cancer*, will make a difference. I have already witnessed these stories impacting others the way I envisioned.

One thing I know is that having family and community around you—people that understand where you've been and where you are going in this journey—can make this diagnosis easier to bear. A great example of this is one of the reviews we received from a young lady:

> "What a great book to read for someone who has cancer or knows someone. I sat outside after revision surgery just now and read the whole book. I love that it was short stories and that there were sisters like me."
> **This is exactly what I wanted to accomplish with that book!**

So how can you turn your story into a movement?

First, you want to establish a vision, goal, or response. What is it you want to accomplish to move your message forward? Second, you want to surround yourself with people who understand your vision. They can be people who have been in your shoes, mentors, coaches, doctors, nurses, or support groups who relate to your message and want to make a difference. Finally, know what action you want others to take to keep the movement moving forward so it has optimum impact.

But it all starts with a story, with sharing your message, with taking the chance and being vulnerable.

Will you join The Silver Lining of Cancer movement?

My goal is to get *The Silver Lining of Cancer* into waiting rooms, support groups, and in the hands of people around the globe who are facing a life-changing diagnosis that impacts them and their families. If you know of anyone, any corporation, or any association that can help us make this happen, I would love to hear from you.

Tracey Ehman is a bestselling author of The Silver Lining of Cancer *and a social media strategist who tripled her business while battling cancer. Her ability to concentrate on the positive, even in adversity, compelled her to bring together others to share their stories and inspire people to look for the silver lining.*

www.thesilverliningofcancer.com

STEP OUT, STEP IN, STEP UP

Charmaine Hammond

Life is full of moments: moments that define you. Moments that shape you. Moments that challenge you. And moments that help you grow.

Do you recall as a child what you wanted to be when you grew up?

Did you have a big dream that lit you up?

Some of you may have been like me, changing your grown-up plans and dreams, and some of you may have become exactly what you decided when you were young. Both are perfect outcomes.

As a painfully shy child, I wonder now if my parents ever imagined I would become a professional speaker and entrepreneur. They may have suspected I would become an author because I loved books, being read to, and writing. Maybe they did believe I would become a speaker. After all, I spent hours playing school after being at school.

I grew up in an entrepreneurial family with loving parents, great storytellers, two incredible sisters, strong family connections, and the encouragement to pursue my own path.

That path led me to become a correctional officer. Yup! I worked in jails. At four foot eleven and three-quarter inches, I didn't look like the "typical" jail guard. I had short, spiky blonde hair, a big heart, and a desire to make a difference. This ten-year career working with some of the most challenging adult and youth offenders taught me so much, including the ability to ask for help, be humble, recognize that everyone has a story, and realize that who they are in a particular moment may not be who that person actually is. This career taught me perseverance, the power of kindness, and how to cope with failure and painful learning experiences (there were many).

Ten years after I left the correctional system, I returned to school to earn a BA and then a master's degree in Conflict Analysis and Management.

I had worked as a counselor, the leader of a youth/teen drop-in center, the executive director of a women's crisis shelter, a program director of a psychiatry unit, a contract negotiation specialist for government—and then I was called . . . to step out.

I stepped out of a career I enjoyed that paid well, offered security, and provided me with ongoing learning. But it did not give me a sense of purpose.

Have you ever felt like something was missing? A sense that there was a bigger purpose for you, even if you didn't know what that was?

Purpose was the one piece missing in my puzzle of life. The rest of (or at least most of) the puzzle pieces were there. I had a loving family and husband, incredible friends, a social life, hobbies that gave me joy, and the list goes on. The missing piece was purpose.

Leaving my stable career and venturing into the instability of the entrepreneur world resulted in more roadblocks than I ever expected. However, even in the most challenging moments I never once thought about stepping back. I had stepped in—stepped into my purpose. I opened my first business, a dispute resolution company as I had become a chartered mediator. It grew to a team of five in less than two years, and then I opened my second business, an employment services company that employed five staff members. Now, I might be biased here, but I had the best teams a leader could want.

I clearly remember the day I was called to step in again. A corporate client had asked me to provide their team with some dispute resolution training and help their human resources department set up their internal policies and conflict resolution programs. For the first time in a long time, I was nervous. I didn't trust that I could deliver what I agreed to deliver.

But the moment I stood in front of those twenty team members, all eyes on me, I felt at home. I remember thinking, "*This* is what being on purpose is."

I stepped in. Speaking became my new joy—my new purpose.

Very quickly the speaking side of my business grew, and I mediated less and less; I had a highly capable and committed team to provide that service. I eventually changed my business model to focus purely on speaking, which I now have been doing for many years. My husband and I decided to move out of the community we were living in, resulting in more key decisions. Moving from having two incredible teams, two offices, and two businesses to becoming a solo-preneur was a big change. I found myself seeking opportunities to partner with other businesses or organizations, to collaborate with them on projects, products, or programs. Collaboration lights me up.

In the process of stepping into these big life and business changes, I found myself quickly being invited to step up—to step up and support projects that matter, be a part of movements that make a difference, and utilize collaboration to create bigger impacts . . . which is the mission of Raise a Dream, a business I co-founded with my business partner Rebecca Kirstein.

As I reflect on the past thirty-plus years of stepping out, stepping in, and stepping up, there are three threads woven throughout, almost as if stitched together to support my purpose: kindness, collaboration, and courage.

Kindness is not just about how you show up and treat others. Kindness means giving, including giving kindness to ourselves. Kindness has the ability to transform relationships and lives, and it creates a ripple effect of more kindness.

Collaboration can inspire creativity, make the load lighter to carry, and create results not possible on your own. We always say, "It takes a team to raise your dream."

Courage is necessary for growth, change, stepping out, stepping in, and stepping up.

Life is full of moments: moments that define you. Moments that shape you. Moments that challenge you. And moments that help you grow.

The question is: How will you spend your moments?

Charmaine Hammond is a highly sought-after business keynote and workshop speaker. She is a business owner who teaches the importance of developing trust, healthy relationships, and collaboration in the workplace. Charmaine has helped corporate clients build resilient, engaged teams, develop high trust/accountability relationships, and solve the tough people issues that impact success.

www.charmainehammond.com

Overcoming Obstacles Is Your Choice

Eva Hebebrand

Have you ever had one of those August weekends you just knew was going to be perfect? I had just finished a class for my master's program. My husband and boys picked me up from the campus, and we headed to Los Angeles for a fun weekend. We had planned to spend the night in Santa Monica, going to the pier, having dinner, and enjoying the rides. The next morning we planned to get up and head to a Dodgers game with premier seats and reserved parking. I had no idea that night would change my life forever.

After checking into the hotel, we took off for Santa Monica, where we had a great time on the rides, ate dinner, and listened to a concert. We headed back to the hotel, but we did not make it. I remember our windshield cracking, the car spinning, and the jarring sound of the force of two cars colliding. My right arm had been outside the car window, and that was the point of impact. It had been almost amputated, and there was substantial bone, tissue, and muscle loss. As the emergency personnel planned how best to get me out of the car, I remember thinking, *I will not be defined by what happened in a few seconds over which I had zero control.*

The next ten hours were a complete blur. I went into emergency surgery as the doctors tried to save my arm. Four weeks and eight surgeries later, I was finally released to go home for a few days. My arm had an external fixator attached by screws in my arm bones. Six days later I went back to the hospital for almost two weeks for a skin graft, then back home for recovery. At the end of October, the doctor had a custom cast made to replace the fixator and hold the muscles in place. It was almost three months before I could stand and walk without help. By January, I was able to return to work. However, this was not without its challenges.

Without the use of my right hand, I had to learn to do everything with my left hand. Just as when I was a child, I learned to brush my teeth, comb my hair, and dress myself. The most difficult challenge was learning to write again. It is amazing the number of tasks we do without thinking and take for granted.

I wanted to have my life back, but I quickly realized that was not going to happen. I made the decision to look at what I had, not what I had lost. We all have some type of disability; mine now was merely more visible than others. I didn't have control over what happened to me in that intersection, but I do have control over how I react to it. I had a lot of living ahead of me, and I did not want to miss a minute of it. My faith, my husband, my sons, and my friends were all there to support me.

One of my greatest lessons was learning to be humble. I was one who did things for others, but now, I had to learn to be humble and accept the help of others. I found it a hard lesson to learn because I had been taught it was more blessed to give. I was determined to finish my MBA program, and I learned to let others help me. I dictated papers to friends who would type them, my husband, David, read my textbooks to me, and my son posted my papers.

I have met incredible people on my journey and received kindness and goodwill from strangers in many different situations. For instance, one day I went to buy dog food. We always bought it in fifty-pound bags, so that's what I did. Because I couldn't pick it up, I planned to roll it off the cart into the trunk of my car. When I got to the parking lot, I realized I had driven our truck. The tailgate was too high, and the door was too small. Suddenly I saw three young men coming from different directions to help me.

I have been fortunate to share my story with groups and individuals of all ages. I sat down in a café at the beach one afternoon. I saw a young man looking in my direction, but I could tell he did not want to stare. "How's it going?" I asked. The young man began to tell me about his girlfriend who had recently been in an accident and lost her hand. He explained how depressed she was; she was not sure how to go on with her life, and he wondered what could he do to help. I shared my story. I told him that we must focus on what we have and not what we have lost. His girlfriend still had one hand, two feet, and unlimited possibilities. He could encourage her to identify what she is interested in, what she could do as a career, and head in that direction.

I always try to leave people with three thoughts:

- The way you react to a challenge is your choice. You may not have control over the circumstances, but your reaction is your choice.

- Learn to accept the things you cannot change and adapt. Set yourself on a path for success. For instance, since I cannot tie shoes, I don't buy shoes with laces.

- Find a support system. It may be your faith, family, friends or a support group. For me, it was my faith and family. Change the things you can for the better.

It has been fifteen years since the accident. My life is once again normal . . . my new normal. The biggest lesson I've learned is that what happens to you in life does not define who you are—your choices to overcome situations do.

Eva Hebebrand has been inspiring individuals and groups with her positive message of overcoming challenges for fifteen years. She has worked for international and Fortune 100 companies and has been a university administrator. Now she shares her life strategies as an exciting keynote speaker motivating others at forums and leadership conferences.

www.evahebebrand.com

Good-Bye, Little Girl

Sandra J. Horton

Walking down the great hill, I see the ocean in the distance with the sun radiantly beaming light off its surface. The beautiful peacocks stand majestic along the lower hill as I turn my gaze toward them. Little did I know everything in my life was about to change.

Eyes wide open, an exhilarated feeling flows through me as I wait for the third day of my master's in leadership graduate class at Royal Roads University, Victoria BC, to start. The classroom is a buzz of conversations as classmates get to know each other while waiting for the teacher to begin her lecture. Today's lecture is on transformational leadership, and we are looking more deeply into ourselves after being asked to share an "unresolved story."

I felt an unfamiliar sensation stir deep within me, and my thoughts started swirling in my head like a merry-go-round as I heard my instructor completing her instructions to get started. I impulsively jumped up and ran over and grabbed the two women I wanted to have in my group. One of these women turned out to be very instrumental in how I managed through my unresolved story, as it could have gone one of two ways. Our small group headed out of the classroom into the main foyer to share our unresolved stories.

Walking quickly, we entered the foyer and sat down in the three large, comfy chairs across the room facing the right-hand wall. I am relieved that it is only us in this great open space. As soon as I sat down, something came over me—it was like a fast-speeding train with no brakes crashing out of me as I blurted out my unresolved story. My body start to quiver and shake slightly, and I began to cry as I closed my eyes and covered my head with my hands. I felt one of the women touch my hand, and with an overwhelming feeling of embarrassment, I shared how I had been raped when I was ten years old.

My whole body felt like it was on fire, and my mind was whirling. I seemed to be looking at myself from inside out—from a deep, dark place within myself. I heard one woman asking me something strange. I tried to understand, and I finally realized she was asking me if I was ready to release my little girl.

My mind flashed, and instantly I could see a light shining in the dark. Suddenly I see her, my younger self—my little girl. She is heading toward me and now she is right beside me. I see myself and my little girl standing side by side. It is such an intense feeling. Breathing deeply, I feel strangely calm. A deep acceptance is filling me, and I know I am ready to say my good-byes. I whisper, "I love you," and I know it is all right for her to go now; it is time. In my mind's eye, I see her leave with her left hand raised back toward me. I watch until she walks away out of my view. A pure sense of complete release washes over my entire body as I surrender to what I'm feeling. The power that has held me captive for so long has gone. My younger self has been released. I have found my voice. My life has been made clear. Tears flow down my cheeks in a sweetness only I understand as I return to the foyer. I lift my head and look at my friends who have witnessed this life-altering and profound moment of transformation.

Those powerful personal moments of change provided me with instant clarity. It was vividly clear that repeating patterns of negative thinking had resulted in devastating results time and time again, but I had been unaware of the drivers behind the actions. Intense episodes of loss were caused by simply switching perpetrators, and this resulted in severe physical health consequences and failed relationships. Now I realized that I had never stood up and allowed my voice to be heard, especially when it came to men. Not having my voice truly limited my self-worth and self-confidence. *Victimization* and *co-dependency* weren't words I was familiar with, but I grew to understand that I had lived them in multiple situations throughout my life.

I've come to realize so clearly that by not understanding myself and my life story, I had played out someone else's story. Learning about myself has allowed me to stop, reflect, and challenge my assumptions and my habitual ways of thinking and being. By shifting my focus from outside to inside, I discovered my truth. Exploring emotional intelligence gave me the language to understand myself on an even deeper level. Through powerful reflective practices, I have learned to shift the words I use to describe myself.

While before they were destructive and self-sabotaging, now my words are encouraging and accepting. All of this was accomplished by releasing those hidden and limiting beliefs held by my younger self, my little girl.

Confidently, I now stand tall. I have no need to protect myself from my own fears and those of others. I no longer need any armor to shield and protect myself. I am open to myself, to self-love, to accepting love from others, and I've developed the ability to *give* love to others. Gaining personal insights is both powerful and redemptive. I now find myself living with an open heart, with a sense of gratitude, and with the knowing that the hardest, darkest, scariest times in our lives can teach us incredibly important lessons.

Each of us has the power to shift how we look at ourselves and how we perceive the situations we find ourselves in. I hope my story inspires you to courageously look within and say good-bye to limiting beliefs you may have clung to for years. Perspective is everything, and when you change your perspective, you change your life.

Sandra J. Horton holds an MA in Leadership. She is a passionate crusader on a mission to empower women to know and own their stories. She assists women to unearth their hidden treasures and release their limiting beliefs by guiding them to shift their perspectives and change their lives.

www.womenscollaborativehub.com

Soy Mi Cuento
(I Am My Story)

Lillian Díaz Imbelli

The first time my voice emerged was also the day I lost my innocence. I was only six. We lived in the North Bronx. At that time, the borough was yet to be the stuff of urban legend. Rather, the northern corner was a bucolic haven away from the South Bronx, which was more urban, loud, and bit more gritty. My cherished grandparents (mis abuelos) still lived there, and not owning a car, our family would travel back and forth by subway. We'd emerge from the depths of the tunnel into the light as the tracks climbed the elevated structure above ground. As a young child, I remember feeling delivered and safe. Although I had no words for those feelings, they were palpable. It may have been just a few short stops away, but it was a world apart.

Because of this, we were eager to have my grandparents live closer. So on this particular day, my mother, a young Latina whose Indian roots were evident on her beautiful countenance, and I, her fair-skinned, dirty-blonde-haired daughter, entered the local realtor's office, hoping to make this happen. We were quickly ushered to the back.

My eagerness soon turned to a sense of disquiet. I didn't understand why my normally guarded mother was so forthcoming, answering all kinds of intimate questions asked by this realtor with her high-pitched stutter. Even as a young child, my culture was firmly ingrained in my soul, and I knew without a doubt that family stories were to be guarded and protected—not shared and dishonored in public. The more my mother divulged, the safer I felt closer to the door. I kept hearing the realtor's question over and over in my head: "So, what color are your parents, Sweety?" As tears spontaneously flowed down my cheeks, I blurted out, "They're PURPLE!" and ran out the door, where I felt even safer.

My *abuelos* never did move closer to us, and I came of age amidst the smoldering decade of the seventies. Landlords were paying to have fires set when they discovered insurance would yield a higher paycheck than the going market rate on their aging, poorly maintained rental properties. As the South Bronx burned, a new type of refugee was created. Neighborhoods that were previously settled by predominantly white ethnic groups of European decent felt encroached upon by people of color. Hostilities ensued, and welcome mats were quickly withdrawn.

As a white Latina, I was inadvertently exposed to a unique vantage point. Most newcomers to my community surmised I was not Latina and did not speak Spanish. Old-timers gathered that I was one of them and held the same territorial allegiance to maintaining the status quo: no outsiders welcome. I was unintentionally privy to the most private thoughts of both groups. I heard unsolicited laments about the current state of change and accusations that "those people" were ruining the neighborhood. In Spanish, I would suffer the slings and arrows of a people eager to feel safe in their homes again and perplexed by the hostility greeting them. Lashing out verbally in a language no one could take from them, they defended themselves against more pain in tones that needed no translation.

Decade after decade, my story was often told by others thinking they knew me better than I knew myself. For instance, a college financial aid officer, upon reading a letter I wrote to address an issue I was experiencing, expressed his astonishment at my ability to write and advocate for myself based on his assumption that a Spanish surname would indicate otherwise. What he meant as a compliment, "You can write!" would be called a micro-aggression in today's PC climate. Or the American diplomat to a Latin American country, who upon hearing I would be spending my junior year abroad there was eager to share his insights. He gushed, "You know the best part of this country?" I shrugged, eagerly waiting his observation. "There are no Puerto Ricans!" This comment had a silencing effect on all those surrounding us, but on no one more than me.

When your story is being told over and over by people in power, whether in the media, in schools, communities, or at work, until you no longer recognize it, the initial effect is to silence you. When your culture reinforces that in a subliminal way, encouraging you from early childhood to make no waves, be grateful, take what you can get, guard your privacy, and be good above all, the effects can censor you.

After graduating college, I found myself most at home outside the familiar. I traveled and taught English in Colombia and Japan—first in a Spanish-speaking country where I found a piece of myself, and then in a country that was so new and different that being an outsider was an adventure. While it may not have all been a bed of roses, each of those experiences became a unique part of me.

Over time, I have become comfortable living in multiple worlds. My dissertation research led me to the work of Gloria Anzaldúa and her Borderland theory, and I discovered I was not alone. Many of us are hybrids; we identify both with the culture of our birth and the one in which we live and work. Our stories are uniquely ours.

Discovering my voice was a long time coming. Today, I offer students the tools and tactics to embrace this reality, so that it need not take them six decades to do so. We are our stories, and we all can learn so much if we are open and eager to challenge what we think we know about ourselves and others.

Lillian Díaz Imbelli, EdD earned her doctorate at age fifty-eight, after twenty years in education. Her online course, The Sage Project, offers tools and strategies for Latinas to identify, embrace, and use their hybrid identity to empower their leadership.

soymicuentoblog@wordpress.com

DIVINE AWAKENING WITHIN

Deborah Marie Isis

Wake up! Wake up! I was literally woken up, by spirit, to write my morning pages after putting out a big intention for what I wanted to share as my message for this book. I awoke to the awareness that this message is not for the fainthearted; it is for those who have an inner warrior inside of them waiting to be released. That warrior is waiting for you to wake up to your divine calling and step over the edge of your fears and doubts and confusion—everything that keeps you safe and small and liked and fitting-in . . . or hanging around on the sidelines so as *not* to fit in.

You know there is something different out there for you, but you don't want to upset the applecart, displease people, or piss anyone off because you are scared of the consequences of their wrath. But this is *your* life—you came here to be a sovereign being, living an inspired life and your divine purpose. You are a shining, strong, illuminous diamond at the core of your being, in whatever shape or size you showed up here.

It is time to wake up now to who that is—who *you* are! It is not about what you have in this world anymore; times are radically and drastically changing. It is ultimately about who you came here to be: a radiant, shining diamond self with a point to make in this world. Your point matters; you matter. Your way of being in the world matters. It's time to release yourself from the chains of bondage of the small ego self and allow yourself to shine as the magnificent divine being you came here to be.

When I was experiencing some confusion in my life, a lovely Reiki master friend of mine once told me, "Deborah, you are here to just be love and do love." That rang true for me at a deep soul level, although at the time, it did not sit very well with my ego self who wants to have and know and do and not just *be*! But not long after that, I decided to surrender to the divine within myself—which is not giving up, but rather giving up allowing our ego to control the show. I realized that being love is also what I do in the world, but love isn't always nice—sometimes it is fierce, and that is okay. From navigating my own heroine's journey and travailing deep valleys and venturing into dark foreboding places that are definitely not for the fainthearted, I have discovered my purpose: I came to earth to lead and inspire and motivate in whatever way that presents itself to me and to wake people up to see who they really are.

In the Gnostic Gospel of Thomas, Jesus said, "If you bring forth that what is within you, what you bring forth will save you. If you do not bring forth what is within you, what you do not bring forth will destroy you." I am, therefore compelled to carry out my mission, but it has not been without overcoming major resistance myself.

I was brought up as a strict Catholic believing that God was a man who sat on a cloud, forever watching over us, judging us as good or bad or worthy or unworthy, even innocent children.

I turned away from religion in my late teens, but I always kept my deep faith, which was the blessing my mum (who is no longer on the earthly plane) instilled in me. My interpretation of G.O.D. now is Great Omnipresent Divinity, which is the Divine within us all, our Creative Spirit. This Divine Intelligence is always present and watching over us, waiting ever so patiently in divine timing to guide our lives when we connect with our own Divinity within. Divine energy is all encompassing, lives in us, and breathes through us; Divine Intelligence makes our heart beat and creates a human being from a single cell. That is who we really are, divine powerful beings, although it took me a very long time to wake up to that fact.

I have journeyed through the alchemical fire on my own spiritual quest for over twenty years, after falling into depression following my divorce in my early thirties. In addition to working in the corporate world, my quest included being a paramedic, a social worker, a teacher and trainer, a college lecturer, a single mother, a florist, an entrepreneur, and an intuitive coach. I embarked on a parallel journey of seeking answers to life's big unanswerable questions through training in the modalities of counseling, NLP, Reiki healing, magnified healing, animal healing and communication and journey healing to extensive training in intuition and egoic pattern mastery.

I have experienced phenomenal highs and equally spectacular lows. My life experiences have brought me to my knees and the dark night of my soul. I experienced near-fatal heatstroke. I received a diagnosis where the practitioner told me that she had never seen results like mine unless someone had a terminal illness. I've undergone emergency operations. I've experienced a suspected brain hemorrhage, two almost fatal ambulance crashes, and several other serious accidents. I've been in an abusive relationship, and I've even been homeless.

Through all of this, I discovered that we all have an egoic pattern that wants to protect us and keep us small in the world and plays out over and over again in our unconscious awareness until it is exposed. The last few years have seen my intuitive mastery increase, and I have risen like a phoenix from the ashes over and over again. Now I'm able to assist my clients to do the same with a far-reaching impact. Their heartfelt thanks for assisting them to change their lives is truly humbling.

It was only when I was brave enough to surrender to Divine Intelligence within that I truly awakened to my own magnificence and realized that my mission is to awaken others to their own Divinity within and the divine blueprint for their life. When we awaken to the Divine within, the Divine within awakens.

Deborah Marie Isis is an intuitive coach, connecting people to their divinity within to live an inspired life. Deborah believes the Divine is within us all. With intuitive coaching, training, speaking, and writing, she opens you to the Divine's vision and blueprint for your life and works intuitively with Divine Intelligence to create it.

www.deborahmarieisis.com

DARING TO LEAD!

Pamela Jay

As my father blew out the candles on his ninety-first birthday cake, a wave of terror washed over me. "Oh my God!" a voice inside me wailed. "I am waiting for my parents to die before I share what I've discovered!"

Committed to being available to my parents as they aged, I worked nearby as an estate gardener. I dreamed of sharing with other women something important I had learned . . . someday . . . *after* Mom and Dad were gone. Everything shifted with that birthday celebration, and seven months later I had twenty-two courageous clients from around the world.

As a transformational leadership mentor, I help women entrepreneurs unlock the hidden power of their natural voice and feminine strengths so they can speak with magnetic clarity, lead with ease, and empower others without burning out. I'm known as "The Voice Whisperer."

But I'm getting ahead of myself . . .

For twenty-seven years, I hid something precious I had learned. I was terrified of being judged.

"Who am *I* to say there is a feminine, more effective way to lead our lives and businesses than what our society has modeled? No one will believe me. They will call me crazy. I will embarrass my family. My community will call me a witch and reject me."

I mean, what could a thirty-eight-year-old Indiana farmwife with two young boys—who healed her Crohn's disease by singing in a grain silo and talking with an invisible presence named Sarah—possibly know about the nature of *leadership*?

Weak from pain and severe weight loss, I would sneak off daily to sing quietly in the acoustically rich stone silo. The sound of my voice echoing back felt like warm butter pouring over my aching body. I scribbled down messages that Sarah's "voice" seemed to whisper:

You are sick because you are trying to be someone you aren't.

Remember how you felt when you were eight years old singing in your backyard treehouse? Feel that again. Reverse your energies—this is the feminine way.

I stopped fighting my illness, and instead I learned to see it as a helpful messenger. I sang to my body. I meditated in nature. I imagined sending sunshine to my unhealthy cells, and twelve weeks later, I had successfully "loved my illness to death." My befuddled doctors confirmed that I no longer needed intestinal surgery.

Sarah's messages continued. I was to use the same process to build a business called Wheatfields, a natural arts learning center for children to nurture their connection with nature, imagination, and their inborn strengths. "Start with an empty farmhouse, no money, have fun, ask for what you need, and expect miracles," I penned.

Wheatfields taught children the value of working together and showing them that everything we need is close at hand. For eleven years my staff and I, along with hundreds of community volunteers, offered experiential outdoor programs impacting the lives of thousands of children and families.

My farmer husband missed the "old me" who enjoyed canning vegetables, plowing fields, and tending the cattle. We divorced amicably, but Wheatfields was located on his family farm so it had to end as well. A part of me died there. And so did Sarah . . . or so I thought.

For the next fifteen years I could not find where I fit in the world. I lifted up the visions of others but quickly tired of the competition, push, hustle, and stress. Nothing compared to the ease and joy of leading the feminine way.

Momentarily reinspired after surviving a house fire and losing everything but my songs, I recorded a children's album called *Heart-Shaped Rocks*. It won prestigious awards, but trotting around the country performing on stages for autograph-hungry kids made my introverted soul want to throw up. Everything kept calling me to be unapologetically true to who I really was. But who *was* I now?

I needed nature again . . . and time to listen. I headed for the mountains of North Carolina in my Jeep, and at fifty-nine, I helped design and build a remote, rustic treehouse where I lived for over two years.

There I found Sarah. I sensed her presence among the mosses, the boulders, and the wren-song. One day, I glimpsed her while bathing in a mountain stream. As I leaned in to get a closer look, my own reflection smiled gently back at me—*I* was Sarah now. And she was me.

Was she my higher self, beckoning me all along to trust the still, small voice within me over the ways of the world? I wept to think how she had kept me honest all these years - trusting my inborn feminine qualities of deep listening, intuiting, observing, collaboration, inclusiveness, generosity, balance, and service. The natural beauty I had been seeking was my own!

As my dad blew out those candles, I made a wish too. To stop procrastinating. To create something new, the same way I transformed my body from sick to healthy. The same way I grew my learning center for children— by trusting my intuition instead of worldly ways . . . the feminine way.

So I write now in my cozy "treehouse" studio, not far from my aging parents, creating an awareness that an exciting, fundamental change is unfolding right before our eyes. I spend my days gathering, recording, and sharing the stories of women entrepreneurs who, like me, are awakening to realize that they have been following a silent calling all their life that has groomed them to step up and play a leading role at this pivotal time in history.

Their stories inspire us to honor our inner nature first, to appreciate the wisdom gleaned from our own journey, with all its twists and turns, and remind us that as long as we are living, there is still time to build a beautiful, sustainable, and better way. Together.

The world needs our voices . . . our daring . . . our stories.

Are you ready to give voice to *yours*?

Pamela Jay is known as "The Voice Whisper" among pioneers of today's feminine leadership movement. She helps them unlock the hidden power of their unique "heartvoice" so they can give voice to their stories and step up as the natural, eloquent, joyful, influential leaders they know they were born to be.

www.pamelajay.com

ALONG A PATH TO HEALING

Nelie C. Johnson, MD

Why do people get sick? Can they heal—and if so, how? These were the questions I asked myself a few years into my practice as a family doctor. I was becoming increasingly frustrated and discouraged. Even with the best medical treatment, and sometimes alternative therapies too, my patients were returning to my office afraid of not making it or of their illness coming back and more suffering.

I figured that unless I knew why my patients were getting sick, I couldn't help them. I was trained to manage disease, not heal it. It came as a shock to realize that I knew very little about healing.

Fortunately, I was introduced to and trained with a medical specialist from Europe who showed me the link between emotions and disease. It was an astounding revelation to me. I came to believe—and I have witnessed this in myself and others—that each of us has the inner resources to support our body to heal disease, from colds to cancer.

What do you believe?

What is your view of disease? If you see it as a physical problem requiring a physical fix, your results will likely be limited. In my experience over the last twenty years, you give yourself the best chance for healing when you do more than treat the physical disease. I see the best outcomes when there is an understanding that the physical disease is arising out of the person's whole life experience—reactions, thoughts, emotions, and beliefs of which most of us are only partially, if at all, aware. You need to look for the cause of the disease or illness and find out why it is showing up. It is showing up for a reason. When you understand that, opportunities for healing become possible.

Is your response to fight disease or to heal it? Perspective is everything. Consider that if you are fighting the disease you are fighting yourself because that disease is part of you. The more you fight it, the more stress and the less possibility of healing you'll have. Rather than fighting the disease, consider approaching it with curiosity to understand why it has shown up and what it might be trying to tell you.

The disease is what it is. Recognize it as your reality for the moment. Be willing to take "response-ability" for it. It's not that you are at fault or have done anything wrong, but rather the disease is the outcome of an unconsciously held pattern of stress and limiting beliefs.

Consider that disease is a sign showing you where your life is out of balance and needs attention and correction. With this perspective disease is giving you a chance to sort out your life.

Many diseases are scary—such as cancer or MS—because they are viewed as progressive and potentially fatal. In actuality, however, all diseases are dynamic events that can progress and regress depending on the energy that drives them—whether stress (fear, guilt, anger, feeling betrayed, self-depreciation) or harmony (forgiveness, love, compassion, self-appreciation, gratitude, peace, joy).

Your journey along the path to healing is your own, but you do not need to take it alone. There are many people who can support you, give you guidance, help you when you feel lost, and encourage you to find your inner resources for healing. I believe each of us is our own healer and possess the power to create health and joy in our lives.

Here are the first steps along the path to healing:

Get a handle on your fear and distress. Receiving a diagnosis of a serious illness such as cancer brings up fear and worry, even panic. It is vital to move on from this stage. Your fears are for a future that does not have to happen.

In facing fear, your best response is to pause and breathe, slowly and deeply. This allows you to be present and calm your fears, bringing more oxygen to your brain so you can think more clearly.

Much of your fear is the result of a lack of knowledge. Consider your fear a signal to gain knowledge and learn about possibilities. Calm, clear thinking will help.

You may be familiar with the acronym for FEAR: False Evidence Appearing Real. Here's another: For Everything A Reason.

Develop an attitude of acceptance. This is your reality *for now*. This is not an acceptance of the prognosis or any projection of a negative future. Your future will depend on how you respond to the present.

Wishing things were different, resisting the reality, or fighting it only fuels the problem and creates more stress. Remember, what you resist persists.

Begin to be aware of your feelings and thoughts. Remember how you felt before you knew about the disease, and reflect on how you felt and thought since your diagnosis. Your thoughts and feelings will guide you to where you have been holding on to patterns of stress and limiting beliefs. These patterns reflect your level of inner well-being.

Be open to understanding that the illness has shown up for a reason. It is calling your attention to aspects of your life that need to be reset—mentally, emotionally, and spiritually. What about your lifestyle might require changing?

When you understand that disease arises out of your life experiences and when you take ownership of how you have responded to them, you empower yourself. You are the only person who knows the impact of those life events. You are the only one who can shift how you react, thus changing the energy pattern of your thoughts, emotions, and beliefs.

You have the knowledge for your own healing journey, although like most people, you need support to access it. *You* are the expert you have been seeking for your healthcare team.

Here's to your health and healing!

Nelie C. Johnson, MD, is a retired physician. As a healing consultant, she brings her extensive experience to empower people along their own healing path through her speaking, writing, and private and group mentoring. Watch for the launch of her upcoming book The Healing Message of Illness *in fall 2019.*

www.awarenessheals.ca

ANTIDOTE TO RACISM

Trilby Johnson

People often mistake me for a feminist, and while I am all for women's rights, what stirs me most is personal empowerment and freedom. This is where we choose to move beyond the limitations of class, race, ethnicity, gender, and age. I consider myself an individualist; I believe this is where the true potential to either create a heaven or a hell for ourselves and others resides. Let me explain.

Over the course of my life, I have often pondered on the fact that I was born in South Africa during the Apartheid regime. I never felt any strong ideological or patriotic links to this country that was supposedly "home." I found that being exposed daily to racism, class distinction, religious fanaticism, white supremacy, fear, hatred, danger, corruption, struggle, abuse, and suffering made me sit up, take notice, and ask lots of questions. I grew up being exposed to many examples of what I did not want in life!

Through my desire to overcome and heal my own suffering, abuse, and struggles, my fierceness for individual freedom and equal opportunity grew. I came to realize at a very young age that there are no winners when it comes to the abuse of power, and specifically racism. Certainly not the victims nor the perpetrators, no matter what anyone may believe.

I have this memory from my first job in South Africa. I was seventeen. I became friends with a black colleague. One day she was talking about how worried she was about her son's health. In my ignorance, I suggested going to the doctors because our medical aid would pay. I will always remember the way she looked at me as well as her reply: "Blacks don't get medical aid, Trilby." I was stunned—and also ashamed. This brought home the ugly truth of racism, and I felt shocked, angry, and saddened at the injustice of this situation. It was simply WRONG!

When we fully realize the destruction of racism and understand that it's morally wrong in every fibre of our being, then things will truly change for good. My own life experience led me to make a deliberate choice about how I want to live my life and find ways to heal individual trauma that can serve as an antidote to racism.

Having experienced inner confusion from the discrimination, fear, and isolation propaganda can breed, I recognize it quite quickly—in myself and others. Werner Erhard speaks about "what we don't know that we don't know." The first step is to acknowledge that we all have the potential to be racist. The difference is how we choose how to manage this fear—because that is what underlies any form of discrimination.

Consequently, informative education, discussion, and freedom of expression is vital around these issues. It is as individuals that we embrace the opportunities to explore and experience states of forgiveness, compassion, and transforming fear. And for this to happen, healing and self-love are imperative!

My life began in an environment of fear and hatred and danger. Contrary to others' ideological and religious aspirations, these facts inspired me to make personal choices that have led me to confront and embrace my shadow self and step out into light. At some point—amidst the despair, depression, burnout, being broke and broken, suicidal tendencies, anxiety, and the distress of not feeling OK being me—I chose to let go and let love instead.

As a native-born South African, I've experienced verbal abuse and attacks for this in Switzerland and New Zealand. It's as though people held me personally responsible for all the racism, without even stopping to ask questions first and hear me out. It's been challenging to defend myself because of where I was born. This has helped me to be more open-minded and less judgmental when dealing with all people. And isn't labeling someone also a form of racism and discrimination?

It's taken me many years to let go of the shame I felt because of where I was born. I learned so much of what I *didn't* want from life in South Africa that today I am grateful for this experience. When we allow hatred to fill our hearts, we become blind to the beauty of life. That's the purpose of racism—to estrange and denigrate. I chose to live life with my eyes wide open to all of life and love.

There's an adage that says, "We blame society, but we are society." I know from my own healing path that finding an antidote to racism is a personal endeavor. It requires us to face and yet embrace all the hidden parts of ourselves that we fear and have judged and discriminated against as wrong. This antidote is an invitation to accept our own personal power and greatness, not arrogantly or as superior, but through self-love, awareness, and compassion. To those living in fear, this can seem like losing control, almost suicidal. Yet the opposite is true; inclusion is so much more expansive for all.

I am passionate about the body and everything that it can do for us. I love the simplicity of our bodies and their straightforwardness—bodies never lie. So when I worked on activating my own and my clients' DNA and releasing of cellular and ancestral energy, I was amazed at the often miraculous healing that occurred.

Today, it's possible with an ancestry DNA test to find out more about our origins and roots. What's striking about the results is their diversity. Mostly, they show how we all come from the same small gene pool. Here is scientific proof that racism or discrimination of any kind is fundamentally self-denial!

I know that racism can be transformed, and once embraced, genuine self-love is an effective antidote to racism. My story serves as testimony.

Trilby Johnson is a breakthrough mentor, intuitive healer, author, and speaker. Having lived on three continents, Trilby runs her successful business, Trilby Johnson—The Connective, from New Zealand and online. She has a BSc honours in Psychology and has written two books, Fearlessly Alone *and* A-Ha Moments, *both available on her website.*

www.trilbyjohnsontheconnective.com

Your Backstory Leads to Your Purpose

Johnnie Lloyd

Everyone has a "backstory," and that story can put a dark shadow over who you are or try to destroy who you were created to become.

My backstory does not look like the story of someone who has attained the levels of success, leadership, wealth, or education I have attained. It is saturated with blood, sweat, tears, hurt, pain, abuse, hate, orange shag carpet, homelessness, positional power, self-sabotage, negative self-talk, and pretense.

I fought back so I would not die in the process—not because of me, but because of my miracle baby. You see, doctors had told me I would never get pregnant. But devastation replaced what should have been the happiest time in my life.

The next twelve to fourteen months is a blur; I went through a divorce, experienced serious sickness, underwent surgery during which I almost died, was separated from my miracle baby, and was forced to sell basically everything I owned. I made the decision to rent out my house, thus becoming homeless. Yes homeless—with a degree in accounting and a good government job. Through all of this, I learned that it's not about what happens to you; it's about your response.

When I became ill, my father drove fifteen hours to pick up his granddaughter. Now, my daddy was known for sleeping while driving. During that fifteen-hour drive back to his home, my miracle baby would scream if he started dozing off. This was pivotal to healing in our relationship. During this crisis, a window of opportunity for forgiveness, love, and compassion opened up. Extending forgiveness allowed me to heal from my father wound. And it was a window of opportunity, because after my illness when I was homeless, my father died.

Experiencing the pain of not having my daughter with me during my illness also caused me to have empathy for my baby's father and vow to never separate her from him or speak negatively about him. I am not suggesting you or I volunteer for more pain; however, there is truth in the saying "what doesn't kill us makes us stronger."

Being homeless is where the orange shag carpet comes in. One morning I woke up sleeping on that carpet with tears rolling into my ears, with my daughter on my chest. I told myself this was *not* my destiny. I was greater than this!

In spite of my fear, I started looking for a job anywhere in the world. I had nothing to lose—we were homeless. I ended up moving to Japan and became known as a rock star accountant in various organizations. I gained profound influence and power, and I traveled globally. However, I was an internal mess, hiding behind several gorgeous masks (power, religion, leadership) yet hurting profusely inside. Despite my pain, I was helping many by providing phenomenal training and speaking at conferences internationally.

Just because we are successful doesn't mean we are fulfilled. As a powerful woman, I neglected my own self-care. I climbed every ladder in sight, but eventually I came to a crossroads. My next defining moment occurred in a rural town in Georgia where I found real self-love and inner peace. I finally released the pain and forgave myself and others during a three-day spiritual retreat in the woods called "Walk to Emmaus."

At this weekend event, I was introduced to the me I was created to be. I found peace, healing, joy, and so much more. I felt like I was undergoing major surgery, lying on the table unconscious with all my guts spilling out and no place to hide. I had to trust the process, and I had to trust myself. I did the painful work of finding out who I was behind all those masks. Letting go of the pain and unforgiveness changed the trajectory of my backstory and helped me to move forward on my terms so I could create a brighter and healthier future.

This defining moment broke the chains that were holding me back, and I would never be the same. I now had the key to unlock those chains, and I chose daily to stay free. My freedom was dependent on me choosing not to turn back; I learned that my mental, emotional, financial, and spirtual freedom are based on my decisions.

During that weekend I started becoming whole. Whole: nothing broken, nothing lost. My history with all the craziness and foolishness didn't disappear, but it was my history, *not* my destiny. The tears I shed at this point were tears of cleansing, washing, purging, and healing.

Once I found the answers to my deepest questions, I found I had a great purpose: helping others become free. I learned to trust my instinct, build right where I was, and use everything for the greater good of others. I found my power in every painful process. Resilience is not just surviving some horrible thing that happens to you; it's learning to thrive and give hope, direction, and encouragement to others.

My professional focus is women who are executives or mid-level leaders and companies that desire to establish, build, and grow their culture for greater levels of productivity. My passion for growth, development, and transformation comes from my backstory and has led me to be a life learner who sees greatness inside and outside of me. I no longer hide behind any masks, and I have achieved true levels of external and internal success. My purpose is helping others to find answers to their questions and build the life they desire and deserve despite their backstory.

These days I am known as the "Pusher." I desire to push you toward something greater and unlock the power in your own mind. So, dream on, my sister, stop hiding, be aware of who you are, and heal from the inside out. Invest in your destiny to release your legacy.

Johnnie Lloyd is a financial guru, serial entrepreneur, speaker, author, coach, and facilitator. She provides inspirational keynote and breakout sessions that empower women's development and transformation, and she delivers strategies for profitable growth. Her insights engage groups and businesses with the mantra "You Are Fire When You Are Focused."®

www.JohnnieLloyd.com

My Why

Michelle McKinnie

There are pivotal moments in life that redefine one's anticipated direction. Many of us have been in a dark place devoid of light, where it appeared that there were no directions and we were unable to move. This is not our natural state; we are warriors. We are survivors despite any circumstance that comes at us. It becomes a story we are able to share with world.

While I currently navigate toward embracing a sense of peace, I certainly didn't skate through the years. I've suffered through multiple disappointments, including failures, loss, doors slammed, no versus yes, sleepless nights, and worrying about things beyond my control. Over the last two decades, I have been challenged with discovering my "why." This has required mental reprogramming, or what I refer to as "heavy lifting." Confrontation was essential, as was recognizing what was detrimental to my growth and making a commitment to change.

If you were to review my credentials on paper, you'd see that I spent fifteen years in nonprofit organizations, followed by a couple of years in healthcare, working in both direct service and management positions. I'd accomplished the personal goal of graduating with a master's degree in Community Counseling and gaining a clinical license (LCPC)—that's two checks on my bucket list.

Adopting a "self-care" attitude, so I thought, was the "golden key" along with the surface smile and nod that suggested to the world that everything was OK. In addition, I prided myself in sharing those nuggets with those I supervised, often uttering the famous words, "Make sure you take care of yourself." As clinicians, we're trained that filling your bucket allows you to minimize becoming depleted. We can certainly declare anything out of our mouths, but the body is not a fraud. Mine certainly wasn't.

Four years ago, in 2015, I embarked on a career shift to the profit sector—specifically healthcare. Anyone who has ventured into that arena is familiar with the expectations of filling quota after quota. My leadership position demanded a tremendous amount of mental dedication, as it was a newly created position that required workflows, processes, and spot-on implementation. Stressful? Without a doubt! Stress was critical to the success of my duties. Add to this the juggling act: wife, mother, stepmother, full-time worker. You may wonder, "How is that accomplished in an ever-changing climate?" Answer: become a nonstop human engine. Of course, this eventually would take a toll on my body.

Eventually my body shut down, and I was forever changed. I'd been experiencing discomfort in my body, mostly resulting from irregular shifts at work and some physical imbalance. Prior to this day, there were some small indicators from my body warning me to slow down, but I wasn't ready to listen. This included but was not limited to headaches, stomach pains, and disrupted sleep. I continued like a car barreling through the blinking yellow light.

On that fateful day in August 2015, two wonderful RNs rushed me into a taxi and escorted me to the nearest hospital. Finally, after hours in the ER and multiple tests, I was admitted to a private room. Six hours later, I heard a statement that caused me to literally stop breathing. "Based on your test results, we have come to a provisional diagnosis of multiple sclerosis."

What? Why? I thought. The tears welled up, but I mustered up the strength not to cry at that moment. I told myself I didn't want audience sympathy and I'd box it up it and mourn when I was alone. For the next several days, a team of doctors and residents swarmed around me, treating me as though I was some kind of case study.

I was confined to my hospital bed because my motor skills had begun to shut down. I had fallen, like Alice in Wonderland down the rabbit hole; however, I felt as if this hole was bottomless. In that darkened hospital room, my life flashed across the screen of my mind, and I began to replay my story. Only days earlier, I could walk, comb my hair, drive my car, and basically function on my own. Now I was in an infant state, unable to independently care for myself AT ALL. I had minimal vision in one eye, and I could only get around using a wheelchair.

The doctor told me that with autoimmune diseases such as MS, stress exacerbates the symptoms. While I attempted to process this, I was flooded with anger, despair, and sadness. My mind was full of questions: *Who am I now? What do I do next? Why do I have to be that person?* My identity as a mother, wife, and woman was literally snatched from me in a moment.

Little did I know, though, that through all this, I would discover my "why" and live my life on a new level.

Today I'm firmly planted in the place of gratefulness, focusing on wellness of mind, body, and spirit. This humble attitude, coupled with God's grace and prayer has allowed my health to be restored. I'm completely self-sufficient, as I had been in 2015, but I now have a different mindset. I focus forward daily and look back only as a reference. My goal now is to share—especially with women—the ability we have to revise the blueprint of our lives so we can discover our "why" and combine it with self-care.

Here is a regimen that feeds my spirit:

- Spending time in prayer every day
- Staying true to my personal beliefs
- Living my why in my thoughts and actions
- Managing what I eat and developing a healthy sense of nourishment
- Making physical movement a priority
- Being intentional about how I live and work
- Getting enough sleep each night
- Saying no without feeling guilty
- Loving myself
- Serving others
- Learning to laugh often

If my story resonates with you, I encourage you to trust that you, too, will discover your why and live with peace and purpose.

Michelle McKinnie is a Licensed Clinical Professional Counselor (LCPC) and holds a master's degree in Community Counseling. With over fifteen years of experience in the social services field as an educator, supervisor, presenter, and clinician, Michelle is dedicated to helping others improve their lives through education, insight, and change.

www.derorwoman.net

LIFE HAPPENS

Irma Parone

Sometimes our best successes come to us simply because life happens.

I have never been afraid of work. At the age of twelve, I begged my parents to enroll me in cosmetology school. In between school studies, I earned money while practicing hairstyling on relatives in the basement of my parents' home. At age sixteen, I successfully passed my state boards. I then worked in hair salons while completing my high school education.

Around the age of twenty, *life happened*. I had an inner ear problem that prevented me from standing for long periods of time, and this brought my career to a halt. Not sure what I could do, I found a job at a nuclear power station in the security industry. Identifying some inefficiencies in the way training and payroll was administered, I jumped in and created systems and processes, quickly becoming a supervisor. I read every book I could on leadership and continued to prove my worth.

In this security company, all employees were required to qualify semi-annually with multiple types of weapons, from handguns to fully automatic M16s. One year, *life happened*. I failed my weapons qualifications. The certification could not be retaken for three months. I found myself laid off—but not for long. The company created a role for me in administration until I could once again qualify.

After receiving multiple promotions and working in a variety of leadership roles, *life happened*. One of my bosses (who was also my mentor) saw something in me that I did not see myself: the ability to look at both sides of an issue. He asked me to fill the role of Labor Relations Manager for the Region. I accepted the position, and over time I successfully completed a Cornell University Industrial Relations Program to further my competence. I continued to move up in the company.

While supporting our three nuclear plants in Florida, *life happened*. I was asked by an old friend to provide a leadership development course for a background investigation company. The owners of that company aggressively recruited me. After rejecting their offer four times, I finally accepted the role of general manager and gave my boss a two-month notice.

A little over a year later, once again *life happened*. My former boss at the security company asked me to come back. It was a hard decision, but the offer was lucrative, and I could not resist.

I returned to the security company, now as general manager of a large industrial branch office with a 51.8 percent customer retention rate. This branch was rated second from the bottom in all areas, including financials. It was a huge challenge, but in a little over a year, my team moved the customer retention rate from 51.8 percent to 93 percent, and the branch ranking was now near the top.

But shortly thereafter, *life happened*. I was terminated.

I was devastated and confused. I can still feel the wrenching pain in my stomach and the hurt in my heart. That job was my identity. No one is perfect, but I had in my hands documentation that proved my quite impressive (if I do say so myself!) accomplishments. I re-staffed and led a team from the worst customer service ratings I had ever seen in my career (plus terrible rankings in most categories) to near the top, and they terminated me? It made no sense.

Shortly thereafter I understood. When I was approached to return to the company, they offered me a very high salary with bridged benefits. I later learned from a credible source that they needed to cut costs as they were in the process of selling the company, and I was one of the tragedies.

Luckily, *life happened* again, and I was soon approached by another company. I accepted a vice president role, and for the next fifteen years I worked there, ultimately serving as the senior vice president. I stayed with this company until *life happened:* my mother became ill.

Initially, I tried to make it all work. My mother, still living in the same house where I had been born, had the initial phases of dementia and could no longer care for herself. I relocated her to Florida, where she lived six minutes from me. The problem was that I traveled often for the company, and that left my mom even more confused. I called my boss and told him I would give him whatever notice he needed, but I had to leave the company. Two months later I was officially unemployed. I am proud to share that I left the organization with my team at the top of the most important rankings.

Shortly after that, I decided to start my own company, which I named Parone Group. I focus on the areas I love most: customer and employee retention and company culture. I worked when I could, as caring for my mom had to come first. Sadly, her illness took her life about three years after I moved her to Florida. On a good note, it was an honor and joy (in the midst of sadness as I watched her deteriorate) to be with her in her final three years of life.

I enjoy my ability to help others excel in their professional careers, and I continue to learn, even at this stage of my life. Currently I am completing organizational development and speaking certifications. I absolutely love what I do!

Throughout my entire career, I have maintained an ongoing focus on improvement and making a difference. Even with that perseverance, life still happened!

The greatest joys of my journey happened because I was open to the opportunities life presented. I would have not made the transition to self-employment if it hadn't been for my mom's illness. I would have not had the opportunity to work as a vice president if I hadn't been terminated from the security company. I wouldn't have been promoted to leadership roles if I hadn't failed my weapons qualifications, and I wouldn't have left the cosmetology business if I didn't have that inner ear problem.

So be open to opportunity when things go wrong. *Life happens!*

Irma Parone is a sought-after leadership consultant, speaker, and author. A graduate of Cornell University's Industrial Relations Studies Program, she is the CEO of Parone Group. For over thirty-five years, she has successfully helped companies improve company culture, increase customer retention, and reduce employee turnover.

www.irmaparone.com

CREATING A MOVEMENT OF WISE WOMEN ON FIRE TO CHANGE THE WORLD

Sirena Pellarolo, PhD

As former president and co-founder of Women Speakers Association Liora Mendeloff reminded us in her "Invitation" that opened the first edition of *Voices of the 21st Century: Women Who Influence, Inspire, and Make a Difference*:

> We are at a defining moment in history—a time when the world as we know it is transforming into something greater than we could ever imagine. We are moving out of a "survival-of-the-fittest" mindset, in which control, competition, and winning are king, and into a more level playing field, grounded in collaboration and contribution—one with women at the forefront . . . the leaders of the twenty-first century.

I agree 100 percent with this assertion. In fact, this is the vision that has inspired my life and the work I do as a Midlife Midwife, supporting women to move through a necessary portal of midlife transformation (a rebirthing canal of sorts!) to become the Wise Women our world needs today. My mission is to build a movement of Wise Women on fire to midwife a loving, egalitarian, and cooperative way of living on this planet.

As a Midlife Midwife, I'm passionate about assisting midlife women to recover their enthusiasm and zest for life as they readjust their body, mind, and spirit during the delicate rebalancing of their hormonal system. I support them as they release the baggage that has kept them confused and sometimes floating in limbo.

Many times women come to me feeling controlled by external circumstances; they feel betrayed by their bodies and experience the loss of a sense of self. I remind them that they have arrived at a stage in their life when they're ready to shine their own authentic light and participate actively in the birthing of a new way of living on this planet. I tell them that their life experiences and knowledge are amazing contributions to this new era into which we're stepping. Their many gifts and talents are now ready to impact the lives of all those that come into their presence. But this vision will become a reality *only* if they are able to release the baggage they are carrying and reclaim the inner power and wisdom that we as women too often relinquish to "authority figures" (the medical community, the media, the beauty industry with its disempowering ideas about aging, and more).

My personal path toward igniting this passion has been a rocky journey of self-discovery in pursuit of my authentic voice. I was born in Buenos Aires, Argentina, in the 1950s, into a patriarchal society that regarded women as commodities and inferior to men. At a very early age, I became fully aware that in order to identify my own authority, I had to delve deep to recover my inner power and authenticity in spite of external challenges that triggered my insecurities. It has been my mission since that early age to share what I have learned with other women.

I was born into a family of very strong, independent women who loved to gather and support each other. My legendary Italian paternal great-grandmother raised sixteen children at the foot of the Alps, many of whom emigrated to Argentina in a quest for the "American Dream." Fourteen of these children were women, and most of them remained single until their death. One was a monastic nun who joined the convent in her teens. There was Rina, who longed for her lost lover who had been killed in World War II for the rest of her life. Tía María became the lifelong mistress of an influential Argentinian politician. My paternal grandmother, Aída, honored her operatic name by embodying a bigger-than-life diva personality, instructing her grandchildren that grandmas do not knit or bake cookies, but rather spend their time in social gatherings and exciting travels.

After living under a repressive military dictatorship that killed 35,000 youth of my generation, I sought refuge in Europe for a time, and finally emigrated to the United States in 1988 with my then-husband and two young daughters, Paloma and Violeta. I entered a doctoral program at UCLA that jump-started my research about women's empowerment and performance in Latin American popular cultures.

Becoming a professor at both of the California University systems, I acted as a role model and mentor for thousands of young Latina women. From them I learned about the resilience and power of women immigrants who face their own share of challenges. I am proud to have mentored the women-led group of student activists who fueled their discontent about their undocumented status into drafting a bill that was later passed as the Dream Act, which has allowed so many young immigrants to enter the process of legalization into this country.

I have witnessed firsthand the incredible creativity of Zapatista indigenous women from the state of Chiapas in Southern Mexico. Their cooperatively owned handmade textile and embroidery industries help finance their autonomous communities. Their own struggle as women in the Zapatista ongoing road towards self-determination is a revolution within the Revolution.

Finally, I am committed to the Red Road of Native American spirituality. I have witnessed, embraced, and learned from the heart-centered spiritual power of indigenous women from both sides of the US border who, against all odds—even torture and murder—continue to be stewards for change in their communities.

Everything that I've learned from my ancestors, my life experience, my research work, and the example of my fellow immigrant sisters has made me the powerful woman that I am today. I use the expertise I've gained to support women as they navigate midlife transitions in a natural and empowered way. Moreover, I've found the confidence and vision to successfully create my own midlife relaunch from college professor to midlife reinvention coach, where I coach my clients how to reinvent their lives by unleashing their unique personal power, creative self-expression, and hands-on genius in order to courageously embark on the selfless task of changing the world.

Dr. Sirena Pellarolo, Midlife Midwife, is professor emerita of Latin American Studies, a holistic health coach, spiritual counselor, author, and speaker. With over thirty-five years of experience researching women's empowerment, mentoring thousands of students and clients, and facilitating women's circles, Sirena guides women to successfully navigate midlife transitions.

www.sirenapellarolo.com

I Threw Away My
Superhero Costume

Cheryl Peltekis, RN

I can still remember the day I tore off my superhero costume. It was a day like any other day. I got the kids up and off to school, all five of them. Then I made the forty-minute commute to my home health agency office and dove right into my work. That day I had to work on getting my home health and hospice organizations ready for a survey from the Joint Commission of Accreditation, which sets standards for excellence. I focused my attention on completing the performance improvement minutes for the last three years. The last surveyor wrote in our exit survey comment section that our company's performance improvement program was one of the best he had ever seen, and I wanted this surveyor to be equally impressed.

I finished putting the minutes into a PowerPoint presentation, printed out the slides, and was putting them into a binder when my husband and our CEO came into my office and asked for the performance improvement meeting minutes. I gave him the binder, and he started going through it. He said something like "This is good," and then he said things that completely erased anything positive he had previously said. "But I think you need to change this, and I don't like that you documented that, and . . ."

The next thing I knew I was in my mind, watching myself rip off my superhero costume and throw it at him. Then I heard the smashing of glass, and I snapped back into reality. I had just thrown my coffee mug at him. It shattered into a thousand pieces—thankfully he wasn't hit by the mug or any of the broken glass. He looked at me, stunned, as I stood up, grabbed my purse and keys, and left.

That was my last day of being a superhero. I was so tired of having to live up to those false superhero standards. I was tired of always having to be perfect. I was *done* being perfect. You see, for the first twenty-two years of marriage, I chose to do it all. I cleaned the house, helped the kids with their homework, cooked all the meals, and did the laundry because I chose those roles. Why anyone would choose to wear so many different hats, I'll never know, but I had learned a set of rules that required me to be a superhero at all times—to be perfect in every way or be considered a failure. It may have started when I was only eight years old and my brother was killed by a drunk driver; I remember being told to be strong, don't cry, do everything yourself, and don't be so needy. But whatever that set of rigid rules stemmed from, I knew that I wanted to be treated like a person and not a robot that just did it all as expected and never needed or asked for anything in return.

That night, my husband came home from work and asked me what the heck was going on. I told him he could have me as his wife or his business partner, but he couldn't have both. I also told him that I was through living up to my own self-imposed superwoman expectations. I was extremely grateful and relieved when he said he would rather have me as his wife if he had to make a choice, and I immediately started my own business the very next day. I also signed up for therapy to help keep this false identify away forever and fully remove the costume that hid the real Cheryl.

My therapist discharged me after three or four sessions. She was amazing. She basically told me, "Welcome to the human race. You no longer must be perfect. You can just be you." She shared one last little secret with me. She handed me a lipstick and an index card with the words "You Are Enough!" She said, "Go home and write this on your bathroom mirror, and write it on all of your kids' mirrors too." She also shared some exercises that would help me to love myself, and she gave me a list of books to read. But she basically said, "You are cured. You have returned to the human race, and you are perfect with all of your imperfections."

I share this story with you because I know there are millions of women around the world who have what I call self-imposed superwoman status. So many of us take on the responsibilities of running the household and working full-time, and we think we are failures if we can't get it all done correctly. As I speak about this on stages around the country, so many women have shared their stories with me about how they, too, tore off their costumes and stopped being superwomen. When you too realize that you are enough, your life can become full of happiness, acceptance, and you can achieve unsurmountable success.

First, take a survey of where you are in your life. Are you living by rules that were passed down by your ancestors or your culture? Are you living as a perfectionist instead of a healthy striver? Are you putting self-imposed stress on yourself? We face enough stress in life without putting more on ourselves. The first step toward minimizing your self-imposed stress is realizing how you might be making things harder for yourself. You need to be your own strongest ally and take time for stress relief without feeling guilty. Practice saying no! It's OK to not volunteer for everything. Take time for yourself, even if it is just twenty minutes a day. Stay present and live in a state of gratitude—and be thankful for your ability to live each day to its fullest . . . just as you are.

Cheryl Peltekis, RN, is an established leader in the home health and hospice industry. A bestselling author and popular conference speaker, Cheryl has appeared on television shows around the country to discuss senior issues. And as a mom of five, she knows how to run a winning team!

www.homecaresales.com

OUR CRISIS IS A BIRTH

Shawna J. Pelton

Tune into the daily news, and it's plain to see that our world is at an impasse; humanity as a whole is facing its greatest challenge in recorded history. Many of us feel powerless as our personal lives and environmental and social systems are collapsing in front of our eyes. We're being called to think and act differently about our problems, or risk losing what we value most: life itself.

Do we have the power to bring peace and purpose back into our own lives and influence the natural forces that govern our shared reality?

I emphatically believe that we most certainly do!

Through understanding how universal laws operate, I've come to accept the fact that these uncertain times provide us with the greatest opportunities for growth. Instead of turning away from or attacking the things we most fear, we can rise up and take new action, individually as well as collectively.

In doing so, we gain the ability to see things through a wider lens of possibilities rather than staying stuck in the limited state of resignation.

But first, it's important to evaluate where we've been and own our part in how we got here. The former US Surgeon General Vivek Murthy believes that "what we are suffering from is an epidemic of loneliness." Wisdom teachings say this comes from being separate from our true nature of wholeness.

When disconnected from our essential nature, isolated by self-doubt and fear, it's easy to see why people believe they're powerless in the face of challenges. Living life this way would make anyone feel skeptical of new ideas or people and want to abandon their post.

However, giving our authority away means that someone else is left with the burden of fixing the problems we've created and inherited. Surrendering our sovereignty enables tyrants to have more power, which doesn't serve the greater good. Denying our part is no longer a viable option. You see, we're not punished for our mistakes—we're punished by them.

We are the ones we've been waiting for, and now is the time to claim our endowment. Now is the time to remember who we are, learn how to love, and live in harmony with life.

I'm no stranger to hardship. I was barely twenty-one when I was schooled on its true meaning. After my son's father lost his battle with addiction, I felt as if I was cast into the role of a struggling young single mom, imprisoned by the demons of bad decisions rooted in low self-esteem. Having spent years consumed by darkness, my soul suffered under the weight of unbearable physical, mental, and emotional illness brought on by my own naiveté.

Self-absorbed, I had a hard time thinking of anything but my own problems. I was addicted to a destructive way of seeing, feeling, and acting in life. Then one day, while looking into the innocent eyes of my young son, I realized that he was going to model himself after me on how to navigate through life's inevitable obstacles. If I gave up on caring about myself, what would become of him?

I knew I needed to set a better example about how to live life to the fullest for my son's sake, if not my own. Even though I had no clue how it was going to be done, where to begin, or where it would take me, I was determined to find a way.

I knew that people were living happy, healthy, and viable lives somewhere in the world, even if not in my immediate field of vision. I thought that if one person can live that way, then there's nothing stopping me from being that way too except myself. So right then and there I made the decision to break the habit of being miserable.

Once I made a wholehearted commitment to step into my true identity, with a little . . . OK, a lot . . . of resourcefulness, I was made aware of something quite profound.

The moment you come to a choice point in life, with an acute awareness that it's time to act, a spectrum of possibilities opens up for you to choose from. Think of it like rivers or streams of consciousness that merge with and run parallel to the current channel you operate from. When you jump into that new stream, you are supported by the universe.

Life is always evolving into higher more organized states of consciousness from which to experience itself, and as we (our separate selves) move into that flow of life, it always leads us home (wholeness).

In this world of illusions, people are searching for a real way to become greater than their suffering. Our quest is to activate it from within and remember that we are creators who are here to manifest our hearts' desires. The answers we seek can be found within the nature of our challenges.

A great visionary, Barbara Marx Hubbard, says, "Our crisis is a birth." We are living in opportune times to make a quantum leap beyond our old separate independent and painful self-identity toward working co-creatively and in harmony together to create change for the greatest good of all.

I believe that when people reclaim their power this way, the world will know peace, and I have dedicated my life to serving those on this journey. I hope you'll join me!

Shawna J. Pelton, creator of QuEST (Quantum Evolution & Soul Transformation), is dedicated to making a positive impact on the future of our world through empowering individuals, high achievers, and organizations to unleash their true potential and create a positive personal shift for reducing fear and uncertainty in a world of rapid change.

www.ShawnaPelton.com

THE MYSTICAL SCIENTIFIC PORTAL CALLED MOUTH

Dr. Kalpna Ranadive

I was five years old when I innocently summarized the journey of life into two breath sounds: *"uuhhhh"* and *"aahhhh."*

My mother, an OB-GYN maternity nurse, and my father, a medical records officer in charge of the accurate issuance of birth and death certificates, worked in the same hospital. Ever since I had been two years old, they would routinely bring me to work after school. By age eight, I had begun to volunteer by helping doctors, nurses, and ayurvedic naturopathic practitioners. By age twelve, I was helping in the ER, witnessing life and death in its most raw and vulnerable form.

What I realized when I was five, I finally understood at age twelve. As human beings, we all inhale our first breath of life with a gasped *uuhhhh*, and we all exhale our last breath of life with a nonresistant *aahhhh* through a portal called Mouth. This key realization set the stage for rest of my life.

Growing up in India, my parents made sure I got hands-on experience in the authentic Indian culture, spirituality, and richness within Ayurveda. At seventeen, I was among the youngest to be admitted into dental school, and I completed my master's degree as a periodontist by twenty-three. While my classmates were busy learning dentistry as a specialty of the mouth, my mind was busy connecting the dots between the mouth, body, soul, emotions, source, and beyond. My childhood experiences had trained me to look at the mouth as a portal connecting our inner and outer worlds. As I shared these insights, my patients started to see the connection and began self-healing faster than my colleagues' patients.

In 1999, little did I know that I was destined to immigrate from India to the U.S. While my fascination toward mystic vastness via the mouth continued, coming to the U.S. gave me a fantastic opportunity to use technology to accelerate healing and preservation within the mouth.

Owning my company has allowed me to carve out a whole new practice model designed to create a win-win for both the patient and doctor. Teaching and educating patients about the connection between mouth, body, mind, and beyond became the epicenter of my practice.

Over the past twenty-five years, by cherry-picking the best of Eastern wisdom and blending it with modern technology, my clinical outcomes evolved. Extractions, crowns, and implants were used as an absolute last resort in my practice. Over time, a 99 percent reduced probability for root canal treatment and controlling gum disease with minimal to no surgery became the norm. Patients began appreciating the value of understanding why disease occurred and then working systematically toward eliminating current and future disease trends in their mouth. Patients who implemented integrative healing protocols are now 90 percent closer to health than to their disease. Best of all, it is all scientific, and my practice grew while I was saving teeth.

The success within my practice has empowered me to believe that knowledge has power, and when it is used to do good, not just one but many people benefit. Unfortunately, today's healthcare model is designed to make people give away their power of healing to an outsider. The reality is that no doctor, healer, fairy godmother, or Tinkerbell can heal you! Only your body can heal itself. Others, including you, merely assist the body to heal itself. The mystical creative Intelligence that provided tools of self-healing in the plant and animal world has also provided each of us with amazing tools of self-healing, free of charge! All we have to do is learn about these tools and start using them.

The majority of our body works on autopilot, without us telling it what to do. There is one portal, however, where, our mystical Creator gave us complete and total freedom of "conscious free will"—our MOUTH! The mouth is a powerful and vibrantly vital portal of life!

Think about it: barring criminal intent, no one can force what goes into our body via our mouth, and no one can force what comes out via our mouth in the form of words and communication. The good news is that we are in total control of our mouth. The bad news is that, out of sheer ignorance, we end up abusing the unlimited healing potential in, around, and through our mouth.

How can we consciously tap into the healing powers of the mouth? Through knowledge and systematization! We first learn the "how to" steps from those who have mastered the mouth's wisdom, and then we systematize it based on our individual unique identity.

- Look at the mouth as a "mystical and scientific portal" with unlimited healing powers. Harness the hidden wisdom within waiting for you to maximize it.
- Realize that the structures within the mouth, apart from nourishing, help in balancing and aligning your body as a whole.
- Realize that your tongue is the beginning of the digestive system. Learn to use its constant communication signals with your gut and brain to then heal you continuously.
- Understand how your food cravings, felt in the form of taste, can heal or sabotage your body.
- Go beyond and tap into how what comes out of your mouth in the form of words, air, wisdom, breath, yawns, and more can heal or harm your inner and outer world communications.
- Finally, learn the art of cherry-picking the best wisdom from ancient sciences and blend it with modern technology to create your own individualized health toolkit.

Remember that your choices determine the quality of the consequences and outcomes in every aspect of your life. However, it is never about choices only—it's also about creating your own customized self-healing toolkit. This toolkit can heal not just your body, but your mind, wisdom, soul, and emotions.

And remember, between your first breath of *"uuhhhh"* and last breath of *"aahhhh,"* you have the power to choose and shape your life via your mystically scientific mouth.

Dr. Kalpna Ranadive, DMD, NMD, MDS, IBDM, is an Integrative Biologic Dentist and an American Board Certified Naturopathic Physician. She brings the depths of her unique expertise in ancient wisdom from across the globe, especially Ayurveda, and blends it masterfully with modern high-tech digital dental technology.

www.drkalpna.com

ANYTHING IS POSSIBLE

Donna Rae Reese

Last year I contributed a chapter to *Voices of the 21ˢᵗ Century*. My chapter was titled "The Best Is Yet to Come." It opened by asking: If you were told you had months to live, would you be living your life differently? I asked this after losing two sisters tragically in a matter of four months. I started to evaluate my own life after that, reflecting on all the obstacles I had overcome, and I started living with intention. Living with intention meant living with a strong will of having and achieving everything I set my mind to.

I have always been a strong woman. I contribute this to being the youngest of nine kids. In my early twenties, I bought my first business, which was in a very male-dominated industry. It was hard enough being taken seriously as a twenty-four-year-old, let alone the fact that I was a woman. The challenges that came with that experience thankfully molded my will and tenacity, which would eventually play a pivotal role in literally saving my life.

When writing my chapter for the first *Voices* book, I started having breathing issues. I chalked it up to allergies and the humidity during the hot summer days in Orlando, Florida. My gut (a.k.a. intuition) was telling me all along that it was something more, but I simply chose to ignore it. Five years prior I had been diagnosed with Interstitial Lung Disease (ILD), a disease with no known cause that attacks lung tissue. According to Google I should have been dead within five years. It did scare me nearly to death because in 1970 my dad died just two weeks after my fifth birthday from complications of an undiagnosed lung disease. He died of a heart attack from the stress that his damaged lungs put on his heart. Thankfully my focus was not on this rare disease as much as on the degenerative disc disease that had plagued me for years before that. After the first year with

ILD, my situation improved without explanation, and I nearly forgot that I had it.

In August 2018 my fear from that gut instinct was confirmed. I had just reached the five-year mark with ILD, and not only did it come back with a vengeance, it brought a friend called pulmonary fibrosis! On October 15, I sat in a Florida transplant hospital being given the horrifying news that I had twelve to eighteen months to live without a double-lung transplant. The next bit of news delivered to my partner, Don, and me was the mortality rate of lung transplant recipients. It wasn't good news. Here I was, actually being told that I was on borrowed time—the same platform that I used to make people think about how they were living their day-to-day lives.

As Don and I walked out of the hospital that day, I swore to him that I was not going to be among the statistics that don't live beyond five years. I'm not going to lie; I did feel sorry for myself long enough to say some pretty unforgettable things that couldn't be taken back. I got into the car and called my two sons. I told them the news was bad and then I went on to say, "If I die without attending at least one of your weddings, know I died with regret!" Those were big words for two men that weren't even engaged at the time to hear.

I have never been a fan of losing, and this was not going to be an exception. Quickly I started researching alternative options to help heal dying lungs, and I stumbled upon stem cell therapy. I've known people who have survived cancer and even had knees restored from stem cells. I spoke to my pulmonary and rheumatology doctors, and they both came back with very derogatory reactions. I then asked my lung transplant doctors if it would disqualify me if I pursued it. Their response was "No, but you should investigate it because it's expensive and might not work." A double lung transplant runs well over a million dollars and might not work either. I took a chance and invested in myself. Was the money for the stem cell therapy better served in my lungs trying to save my life or going to the grave with me? Within a week I was at the Lung Health Institute in Tampa, just an hour from my Orlando home. At the time I started the stem cells, I was on oxygen 24/7. While doing pulmonary rehab workouts, I required upward of six liters of oxygen while simply walking on a treadmill. I literally felt as if I were drowning.

On January 21, three months into a twelve-month death sentence, I had my pulmonary tests repeated. Much to my doctor's surprise, my numbers had held steady. I chose not to tell the lung transplant doctors about the stem cell therapy because I wanted an objective review. Three months more passed, and I went for my six-month testing. The tech gave me my test printouts. I quickly compared them to the last two sets, and the numbers were very different. I texted my sons and Don and told them that I was either in big trouble or I was living a miracle. Guess what—my miracle happened! The lung transplant doctors closed my file that day, completely perplexed, saying I was no longer in need of their program!

My message to anyone reading this is that you cannot allow the opinions of others to become your reality. Anything in life is possible—I'm living proof! (On a side note, my sons are getting married this July and August. They wanted to be sure I would be alive to attend; little do they know that I intend to rule the dance floor!) One day my grandkids will be sitting on my lap, and I will share with them my secret of how to make their dreams become a reality.

Donna Rae Reese has had an interesting and full life as a mother, entrepreneur, community leader, and publicly elected servant. Today she is semi-retired and living in Florida. An author, speaker, and coach, she helps others face their challenges with tenacity and a will to win by sharing her Mindset 2 Millionaire message.

www.donnaraeinspires.com

Don't Just Plan for Your Wedding—
Prepare for Your Marriage

Felicia Rickards

It was an absolute train wreck! Then again, I knew it would be. On the rare occasions I binge-watch a reality show, I explain to my teenagers that this is my train-wreck moment. I already know the impending disaster, but I can't look away! One of these shows is "scripted" around couples who are engaged to be married. I watch in awe as they grapple with the reality of cultural differences, parents who launch into a shouting match anytime they are in the same room, the realization that rearing stepchildren is not what they really want to be doing with their leisure time, and a litany of other relationship issues that one would assume had been discussed *before* deciding to plan a wedding.

In today's modern society—where the average cost of a wedding has skyrocketed to over thirty-five thousand dollars—many couples seem to forget that the wedding is merely an event, not a marriage. As the world has modernized, the approach to the process of uniting in matrimony has remained largely unchanged. However, the journey a married couple takes is vastly different than the male breadwinner/female homemaker path of the now-distant past. Despite all the additional expenses, the divorce rate still hovers around 50 percent. If you think of this from an investment perspective, there is a 50 percent chance that a thirty-five thousand-dollar investment will be lost!

By adopting business principles acquired during my corporate career to my coaching practice, I've experienced a change in ideology regarding what success is. I no longer see it as a single, seismic event. Now I define success as a series of actions that, when executed, create momentum and progress while building satisfaction in the process. I would argue that this is why when many people accomplish a single achievement, they still feel that more is on the horizon to be gained. In a similar fashion, a wedding event is not the success. The fairy-tale scenario of the prince and princess exchanging vows under the cloudless sky in perfect designer wear in front of a well-behaved bevy of friends and family is unrealistic! In fact, the end-of-day fatigue, family discord, and event mishaps can leave the newlyweds quite underwhelmed.

Let's modernize the definition of *marriage* to include "two people developing a mutually respectful relationship over time." This removes the pressure of living up to the myth of a single perfect moment in time. At the same time, it creates a realistic famework for sharing a journey through life together.

The outdated marriage preparation process could use some modernizing to support this new reality. Most wedding preparation courses cover five subject areas: communication, commitment, resolving conflict, keeping love alive, and shared values. While each of these do play an important role in any relationship, they could arguably be considered abstract. Unfortunately, many of these programs can create discomfort as their role-playing scenarios attempt to define what each party would do if presented with a given scenario. The reality is, we don't know! Life simply isn't like this. We have no idea how we will react in the future if presented with a challenge, so these exercises are unrealistic.

Two dominating factors affecting the modern couple are living in a society that thrives on instant gratification and the visual bombardment of what success should look like (courtesy of social media). Here are three ways these can be managed in the marriage preparation process:

1. Based on what you know now, where will you start? The process of "adulting" (a term borrowed from my teenage daughter) requires the couple to start planning a few immediate projects. These might include changing their residence, setting up bank accounts, choosing insurance, making their wills, deciding on employment, and so on.

2. Strategy planning and vision boards are not just for companies. Instead of mindless scrolling on social media—which, by the way, has been documented to negatively affect mood and self-worth—couples can spend time establishing guidelines for what their own family goals will be. They will experience the satisfaction of mutual progress as they check off their accomplishments together.

3. Celebrate the small stuff! During marriage prep sessions, couples can brainstorm ways to celebrate often but inexpensively. It's true that our modern minds need frequent gratification, and this is a good way to create regular stimulus.

Back to those train-wreck couples: how could their experiences be different if they had discussed their differences openly and honestly, and then mapped out their core goals together? He likes to work out; she says she doesn't have time. He thought relating to her children would be easy, but they seem so undisciplined. She thought they'd have one big happy family, but neither set of parents has anything in common.

These are uncomfortable, if not emotionally draining, conversations to be having the night before a wedding—and not only then, but for years to come. Some today would argue that marriage itself is an outdated practice. I propose that relationship management techniques have not progressed as society has evolved.

Imagine how much more exciting marriage prep could be with a clear blueprint crafted to guide the new family through life's common turning points. There are no guarantees in life and circumstances are subject to change; however, the impact of these unanticipated changes could be minimized significantly. Many of us in the workforce have helped to influence the decisions, products, and success of a company. We've sat in meetings (sometimes far too many) with agendas and minutes to help us craft a strategy for the best way forward. Why wouldn't you use this same approach to craft your personal future? That's why I created the Lifestyle Design™ mind maps to walk people through the process. I sometimes think I get more excited than my clients when we use these as reflection tools to celebrate success and update the plan based on new objectives!

Felicia Rickards is a coach, author, and speaker. Using transformational business-building tools and Lifestyle Design™ strategies, she reignites stagnant businesses and assists her clients to move from being stuck to success. Using her innate talent to see past her clients' struggle, Felicia implements action plans to change their trajectory.

www.feliciarickards.com

HEARING A CLOSE CALL

Jeannine Rivers

The silence in the room was deadly. As I became aware of that eerie stillness, I thought, *But why am I awake? I thought I would sleep and never wake up again!*

My body felt like jello—firm, yet wobbly. *Oh my God*, I thought, beginning to panic, *what have I done?*

Out of nowhere I heard a whisper: "Jeannine, get up."

"But I can't; I can't even move," I protested. Opening my eyes, I saw dimly that the room was tilted to one side, with everything having shifted to the left, including the door to my apartment.

No longer a whisper, the voice demanded, "Jeannine, get up right now and get to the door! You can do it! Go!"

But how? I thought. *I feel so totally warped! How can I possibly get to the door? There is no way I can walk!* I cried out, "OK!" but I still remained on the couch, feeling totally hopeless. I just wanted to sleep, to dream of a time when I felt whole and happy.

And just as I was closing my eyes again, ready to give up, the voice thundered, "JEANNINE! GET UP! COME ON, GET UP!"

Panic and defeat fought within me. Why should I want to live? Something in that call gave me courage to try. Somehow, I rose and took a few steps, fell to the floor, and then began dragging myself toward the door, all the while hearing, "Come on, just a little bit more, you can do it!" Finally, reaching up, I grasped the doorknob, pulled myself to my knees, and holding on to the door, I stood up and opened it. Bright light flooded the hallway. I felt relieved and, strangely enough, safe. Then I fell to the floor. I would lie there, unconscious, until someone found me.

At twenty-one, how could I have seen no hope in my life? How could I have felt so lost and unloved? After all, I had been a child prodigy, gifted with a big singing voice. At age four, I was singing along with television commercials, never missing a beat or a note. By the time I was seven, I knew I was different, a free-spirited rebel with a dream: I wanted to be on the inside of the TV, singing with Shirley Temple, Judy Garland, and the Jackson 5.

I made my dream a reality by holding concerts in our basement for the neighborhood children, singing "Summertime" from Porgy and Bess, dressing up like my favorite Motown stars, and singing along with their recordings. When I was in third grade, I won my first music award for singing "Let's Stay Together" by Al Green. I was a star at my grade school and a star to the kids in my neighborhood.

How could a dream that seemed like destiny turn so topsy-turvy?

When I was ten, my parents became Jehovah's Witnesses. This religious organization controlled our beliefs and actions, and it changed our family traditions. Association with friends and even relatives outside of our religion was strongly discouraged. Education beyond high school, voting, and celebrating holidays was also forbidden.

As a Jehovah's Witness, my thoughts and ideas were so tightly controlled that by the time I turned twelve, I felt sick inside, depressed, and lost. I was a robot in a glass tower, and Jeannine with her music was inside screaming to get out. A break came when I was fifteen and someone asked me to sing for a gathering. I was ecstatic! I gave a stellar performance, and the response from the crowd was thrilling.

Unfortunately, the elders within the Kingdom Hall were not thrilled. They told my parents it was not wise for me to pursue such worldly glorification.

I died inside that day, not understanding what I had done wrong, and I felt both confused and angry. How could I be born with a gift and then be told not to use it? Something told me that was not right. I began to hear a whisper inside me say, "Jeannine, get out! Run!" But how? I was only fifteen!

At nineteen, I took a job at a retirement home and I moved out of my parents' house. It was a culture shock, but it led to my escape. My new lifestyle, including my new friends, violated my religious doctrines. For two years I tried to overcome the mindset forced upon me as a child. Physically I was free, but emotionally I was stuck, trying unsuccessfully to meet my joyful seven-year-old self again.

On Friday, March 29th, 1985, I gave up. I could see no light at the end of the tunnel, so I took thirty Amitriptyline tablets, 75 mg each. The hospital summary reads: "Her mental status upon admission was apparently confused, disoriented, which eventually degenerated into a coma lasting one week."

No one knows how long I was lying in the hallway unconscious before I was found, but I will never forget what the doctor told me: "Jeannine, if you had been found fifteen minutes later, you would be dead."

If you Google my name today, you will find a world that never could have happened if I had been found fifteen minutes later. I earned an Associate of Arts degree in Vocal Performance at age forty-eight, and I released my debut CD, "Iridescent October," in 2016. Traveling throughout Europe and the U.S., I have had the honor of performing for millions.

The voice I heard that day in 1985, the whisper and then the shout— "Jeannine, get up!"—is the same voice I heard as a teenager, telling me to escape. Now, at age fifty-five, I continue to hear this voice during the most difficult times in my life. I hear that call as the voice of God, reminding me to get to the door and open it because on the other side there is a bright light filled with many more amazing opportunities.

Jeannine Rivers is an inspirational speaker, empowerment coach, and professional vocalist. Her mission in life is to inspire, enable, and motivate people to move out of the darkness and enter a world of exceptional greatness. She shares her authentic heartfelt stories, life lessons, and knowledge with the goal of stimulating positive change.

www.jeanninerivers.com

THE POWER OF WORDS

Eydie Robinson

Remember the old saying, "Sticks and stones may break my bones, but words will never hurt me"? For a long time, I tried to convince myself that statement was true, but I quickly learned that it was FALSE! Words *do* hurt, and they also have power! And I am not referring to words spoken by other individuals—I'm talking about the words we say to ourselves. More than any other words, they can harm us and hinder us, killing our self-esteem and destroying our confidence.

How often do you take the time to really listen to the words you speak? Are you speaking life into yourself or are you speaking negativity? Keep these questions in the back of your mind because my hope is that by the end of this chapter you will understand how your words can change the entire trajectory of your life, transforming you from hopeless to hopeful, faithless to faithful, and insecure to confident.

The dictionary defines *words* as single, distinct, meaningful elements of speech. Just by definition alone, words are powerful. *Distinct* and *meaningful*—those two words say a lot. Now think about the phrases we commonly hear people say, such as:

"I can't"

"I am not . . ."

"That's impossible!"

"If only . . ."

"I don't deserve_____."

Do any of these phrases sound familiar? I remember a time when these words and phrases consumed the majority of my vocabulary, sometimes without me even being fully aware. However, what's ironic is that I frequently described myself as a positive and confident woman. I was oblivious to the fact that the words I spoke in front of others didn't match the words I spoke behind closed doors, nor did they match the thoughts that would frequently fill my head—and that's where the disconnect happened.

To truly be confident and completely faith-driven, you have to believe what you say not only to yourself, but also to other people. You can't say things like "I know that I am capable of doing such and such," while in your head you're thinking, "How am I going to do this?" or "Such and such will never happen!" It's a fact that your brain holds on to negative words more tightly than it holds on to positive ones. This only makes the negative words and phrases even more powerful, and this in turn usually leads to a negative result. I once heard it put this way: negative words stick like Velcro, and positive words slip like Teflon. It is so easy to grab hold of negative thoughts, while we tend to forget the more positive ones.

There are numerous reasons why this occurs. In my case, I grew up around a lot of negativity, and I also experienced many trials and tribulations that caused me to doubt myself. At times I felt worthless, which prompted me to attempt suicide at a young age. Despite the fact that I physically looked as though I had it all together, emotionally I was a mess.

We as women are experts at this. We hide behind closed doors and wear carefully constructed masks. We suffer alone and allow the pain we feel to influence our word choices. I remember being so low at one point in my life that I would look in the mirror in disgust. I would try to think of something positive, but the negativity stuck to me like that Velcro, and it was a hard habit to break. As a Christian, I even tried reciting Bible verses to prompt me to think more positively, but it didn't work because I didn't wholeheartedly believe it.

Words from other people influence us as well. Their words hurt too, and they can greatly affect how we think, act, and feel. So many of us wonder why our lives seem to be going in a wrong direction; much of it is because of poor word choices. We allow the words we hear to influence us, whether these are words we say to ourselves or hear from other people. Many factors contribute to the outcome of our lives, but for the most part, it all starts with our language. You cannot expect to receive abundance, success, and happiness if you are regularly speaking negative things into the universe. The world gives you what you put into it. If you use positive language about yourself and your ability to achieve goals, then that is what will show up for you. Similarly, if you continuously make statements about yourself or your circumstances that echo hopelessness, incite fear, and nurture anxiety, then those words will shape your reality too. And not in good ways!

So how do you change the way you speak? First you have to know who you are. This may take some time, but without knowing who you are, you won't possess the ability to believe what you are fully capable of. Next, you have to become more aware of the things you say and make a conscious effort to change the words you use. When you notice yourself about to say something negative, quickly replace it with something positive. Making this change will take practice, and you will have to reprogram your mind completely, but it is well worth it. Many of us don't realize that once we change our words, we can truly transform our life. You also have to learn to let the negative things people say roll off your back. You cannot allow someone's negative energy to invade yours. Finally, focus on the present. It's a new day! A new day for you to start a new life because the small steps will get you to the bigger goal.

I hope I've challenged you to really think about the words you speak—the way you speak to yourself and what you say to those around you. And I hope I've inspired you to take control of your words and let them be transforming tools to propel you forward to a confident future!

Eydie Robinson is a published author and speaker who has worked in the higher education field for nearly ten years. She holds a bachelor's degree in Business Management and is currently pursuing her master's degree in Business Administration. Eydie is the mother of three children and currently resides in Dallas, Texas.

www.eydierobinson.com

You're More Than the Roles You Play

Lynn Robinson

It seems as though so many people I come in contact with are going through some kind of transition. For some, it's changes within their family dynamics— divorce, children leaving home, career changes, or retirement. Many individuals I talk to seem to have lost their sense of self, no longer sure who they are and not sure what's next. They've lost their identity.

New experiences and changes are all a part of life. We know this intellectually, but when it comes to experiencing them, it's a different story. Change happens quickly and can be completely unexpected.

There is often a silver lining that is not visible until we're through the experience. I have had many of these experiences, and I know what it feels like to be unsure of who you are or what direction to take. This only happens when we lose sight of our true self—who we are at the core and what we stand for.

I had an unexpected reminder at a time in my life when I was off track. I was in a dysfunctional relationship, living with someone who was highly addicted to alcohol and drugs, which I was naively unaware of.

The only part of my life that filled my heart with love and joy was my children. Before I entered the relationship, I had been a single mom for ten years, and I have only fond memories of my son and daughter and me during this time. I still have the most amazing relationship with both of them.

The relationship with my new partner was very stressful and eventually affected my health. Unexpectedly, I was diagnosed with breast cancer.

The doctor scheduled me for surgery just three days after being diagnosed, so I had little time to prepare myself. I decided to go to a local bookstore to read about cancer and instead came home with books on health and healing. I immersed myself in the books and audio tapes (yes, tapes—that's how long ago it was) and got ready for surgery.

Little did I know that this was the beginning of a new chapter of my life.

During my surgery, I had a life-changing, awakening experience. I was taken into the light and my consciousness merged with this light. As this happened, I was shown that we are all pure love.

This was exactly what I needed to get back on track. When I awoke from surgery, I was filled with a feeling of love and bliss that is indescribable. All the nurses wanted to hang out in my room. The light must have been radiating out. The woman across from my bed who was waiting for her surgery said, "If that's what happens, I'm ready."

It was many years before I told anyone about my experience during surgery, but it propelled me on my path of healing and helping others to grow and evolve and live a happy life. I was inspired to help people change their lives, to be happy and stop striving, and to begin appreciating life and living it to the fullest.

I was drawn to become a Reiki master, a Color Therapy teacher, and a Huna teacher. I believe that we teach what we need to learn, so obviously I had much to learn! I also became an NLP certified trainer, and this became my vehicle for helping others to transform their lives.

The first thing I had to do was end the relationship with my partner. That wasn't easy, and at the time it was very scary, but I did it, and from there everything else was easy.

I realized that in order to change my life to a place of joy rather than fear or resentment, I had to get clear on what I wanted my life to look like. I began to think of my life in terms of the experiences I wanted to have rather than goals. Based on this, I also had to get clear on my true identity—not the roles I played, but who I was at the core and what I stood for.

One reason people are devastated by change is that they identify with their roles as if that's who they are, when it's merely a title, just a role they play. When you know who you are at the core, you can move through challenges with grace. Your core identity is based on the qualities and characteristics you embody. Sometimes they may not be as visible as you'd like, but when you know what they are, you'll find them within.

Knowing who I am at the core has allowed me to make decisions that are aligned with my true self. It has stopped me from being influenced by others, and it has helped me be conscious of my actions and interactions with others. I often ask myself, "Is what I'm about to do or say aligned with who I say I am?"

Three years later, I met my husband, and we just celebrated our twenty-fourth anniversary.

I am blessed with an amazing life, and I believe this is the result of getting clear about my identity and the experiences I want to have in life.

I spent way too much of my life doing my best to tone down my excitement for life, my spontaneous adventures, and my deep knowing that life is meant to be fun and filled with love and joy. Once I acknowledged who I was at the core and connected with my true identity, magic happened.

I started my company, bought a house, and lived in Hawaii, where I was married in a sacred place by a Hawaiian Kahuna. I have traveled to many countries for both work and play. I have gone swimming with the dolphins in the wild, and I've started taking tap and hip-hop dance lessons with my daughter. Family is everything to me, and I'm blessed to see mine often.

I hope you'll take the time to discover your true identity, what you stand for, and what you want to experience in life. When you follow your heart and soul and live every moment consciously, magic happens.

Lynn Robinson is an international trainer, speaker, consultant, and author. She is an NLP master trainer who certifies other NLP practitioners and master practitioners. She also offers personal and professional development programs, her newest being Identity by Design. Lynn's purpose is giving people the mindset and skills to live a conscious life filled with magical experiences.

www.therobinsongroup.ca

It's All About Perspective

Gail Rosenthal

I love watching commercials. I love how products are branded with catchy phrases and bylines that set them apart:

"I can't believe I ate the whole thing!"

"Where's the beef?"

"We're Number 2. We try harder."

"The Pepsi GENERATION."

"The UNCola."

These always make me smile. Branding is marketing's king.

When marketing ourselves, we are taught to create brands designed to make us stand out from the crowd. In business, these brands serve us well.

But what about the brands we pick up in daily life? What about the brands created by the people around us—family, friends, coworkers, neighbors, business associates? Anyone with whom we interact will find traits in us that they use to categorize us and the way we fit in their lives. I find such dynamics fascinating. It's human nature—but sometimes it backfires.

Each of us, even identical twins, experiences the world uniquely. We see things through our own eyes, hear things through our own ears, and make decisions about our beliefs and values based on our personal experiences. So it stands to reason that anyone we interact with will have a unique perspective of us that might not match our own.

I had a very dear friend named Judith. She was a paralegal before the term *paralegal* even existed. She was a really hard worker, smart and funny and kind. She worked for Steve, a sole practitioner attorney, to whom she was devoted. He paid her a ridiculously low salary of twenty dollars an hour—and then expected her to work ridiculously long hours.

After ten years of service, she asked him to set up a retirement fund for her, which he did. After all, how long can you work for someone without planning for retirement? In her words, he made her feel "needed," so she stayed with him, putting up with way too much drama.

About this same time, Judith visited her family in the Midwest. She loved her family and treasured the time she spent with them, but one night she called me in tears.

"They won't stop hounding me about how much I shop and how much I overspend!" she wailed. Judith and I had been friends for over twenty years. We'd shopped together and traveled together, and in all that time I'd never seen her overspend.

When Judith got back, she showed up at my door with her bills and paperwork, looking wildly disheveled and a little bit crazy. She asked me to help her figure out a budget. After going over everything, I sat back in my chair. There was nothing out of line about her spending.

There was no overspending issue. She had an under-earning issue!

As a businesswoman, my perspective was simple: start a paralegal business, charging appropriately. Judith's perspective was different.

She jumped out of the chair and said, "I couldn't possibly charge more than twenty dollars an hour. It's the most I've ever made! I can't charge more than that!"

I can still see the shocked look on her face as I explained that a part-time home-based business, charging what her services were worth, would "fix" her problem and she wouldn't have to change a thing. She refused to consider it.

She wasn't interested in speaking with other small home-based business owners who were doing well, personally and financially. Her opinion of herself went so deep that for her a bigger, brighter world with much more money could not possibly exist. That was the part that broke my heart the most. Judith's opinion was built upon the opinions her family held of her, and she clung to their views. She has since passed on, but it's not too late for the rest of us.

With just a little shift in perspective, we can produce a life-changing effect. It can be minimal—just a peek around the corner, a toe dipped into the water to see what the temperature is like. A tiny movement can have mega results.

Every situation in our lives is both positive and negative and at times much less pleasant than expected or desired. Life can't be sunshine and rainbows and unicorns all the time, but how we look at these situations and how we act on them can.

For example, I detest cleaning toilets. I know… it's so mundane, but they *need* to be cleaned. Having someone come in to clean them is not always feasible, so I do it when I have to. I'm not happy about it, but I am happy when the toilets are clean. As Nike says, "Just do it"—no drama, no fireworks, no emotions.

Take my friend Sylvie. She had a fairly successful home-based business, a happy home life. She confided to me that she felt as if she were simply going through the motions; she just wasn't happy—something was missing. One evening, over dinner and cocktails, she happened to mention that she'd always wanted to write a book about relationships, because her relationship with her husband was so fantastic. It was so out of context, we all just laughed, and went on to talk about other things. A few months later Sylvie uprooted her life to move closer to her husband's family. Her business was still stable, but her life was in turmoil, and her health was beginning to suffer. She took a step back, reassessed her life, and rekindled her passion for relationships, and voilà—a book and a wedding services business were born! Sylvie has never looked back!

Sometimes results make it easier to slog through a dirty job. Sometimes knowing it's done is enough. Sometimes it's just rephrasing things to make something more palatable. Sometimes it's just looking at everything . . . taking stock. You can be happy and still tackle things that don't bring you joy. You can be happy and still not be happy about a situation. Happiness is a choice.

Choose to be happy. Shift your focus. Shift your perspective. Shift your life!

Gail Rosenthal is a hypnotherapist, licensed NLP™ Trainer and coach, mentor, and speaker. She is dedicated to helping make her clients' careers, relationships, and lives richer and deeper. She coaches and mentors globally, and her courses and trainings are jam-packed with information and fun, motivating and inspiring participants with clarity and joy.

www.gailrosenthal.com

WHEN WOMEN GATHER, THE WORLD CHANGES

Laura Rubinstein, CHt

Today was a good day. I was energized. The weather was glorious. The flowers were bursting with color. I had a good night's sleep. I especially know when I'm feeling good because I have lots to share about things I'm excited about. However, not everything is rosy in my life (there's nothing tragic either). But yesterday my husband got into an argument with a neighbor, and he was tossing and turning all night about it. He even worried that we'd have to move, and that brought up all kinds of anxiety about the stability of everything from his job to his retirement. Being empathic, I was very concerned that this situation could become a long-term issue. Trying to calm him down with reasoning and assurance wasn't really working. Luckily, my day happened to be filled with opportunities to connect with some of my dearest girlfriends. In fact, if these powerful female influences hadn't been there, my spirit would not have been lifted enough to rise above and dissipate the anxiety lingering in our home.

First was a morning call with my casual mastermind group. We each typically share the contributions we intend for ourselves, our family, community, and causes. The gift of sharing with those who believe in and support each other created a net of strength and belief in myself. I felt inspired by one member who revealed her global vision for creating sustainable communities. When I shared this with my husband, he seemed interested. It put his attention on something that he values and seemed to ease his stress.

Next I went for a walk with three women friends who are passionate about making a difference in various ways: one with entrepreneurs, one with dysfunctional families, and one with women. We discussed very personal family dynamics and helped ease anxiety for one friend. We had no agenda other than to share and support where requested. The subtle yet **most powerful element** of this day is the **knowing that these women are here for me no matter what.** This energizes my confidence as they are a safe place for my heart to come back to. I like to say they **"have my heart"** like someone would "have your back."

By the time I got back home, I realized that I didn't have to fix my husband's anxiety. Being with my girlfriends naturally quelled my own fear which was being triggered by the negative headspace he was in. I was fortified by my community who I know has my heart whenever I need them.

I went for a second walk later with a dear friend who shared about co-housing training—which was, as it turned out, a great resource for my mastermind friend in developing her sustainable community. I could have thought of this as a simple, sweet day with good friends. However, from another perspective I gained strength just by being with my women friends, and possibilities expanded for me, my friends, our families, and our communities. The synergies and impact made possible included keeping me and at least one of my friends from going to a dark, anxious, emotional place. And this made for two less anxious people in the world. It was just one day and a couple of conversations. Imagine if more people felt that kind of support surrounding them, like a comforting blanket that is always there. Might there be several hundreds . . . even thousands . . . less anxious people in the world? Might it be a different world?

When we gather as women, we often seek advice, connection, and healing. **When we cultivate this connection intentionally with other women who "have our heart," the world shifts**—first in one's inner circle of family and friends, and then the ripple effect takes place. Then it spreads to the immediate community and other communities, and so on.

We've seen it with the "Me Too" movement. In 2006 the phrase was coined by one woman. And in 2017 a hashtag was popularized by millions of women sharing it on social media. A global movement occurred with the collective of women intentionally supporting each other.

We've seen young women such as Emma Gonzalez after the Parkland high school shooting in 2018 ignite the March For Our Lives movement. From her initial request to speak at a rally that was granted by another woman on the school board, she has continued to garner the support of so many fellow citizens. She has gone on to write a book, have a featured *New*

York Times op-ed article (with almost every comment cheering her on). No doubt if women continue to support her, our world will be cleaner, healthier, and safer.

Whose heart do you have? I hope it's every woman who comes in your path. If you see them anxious, if you know they need something, could you ask to help, offer a smile, or simply intention for them a little more love? **When we have someone's heart the way you have their back, we bring healing.** What if we listened from our heart to theirs? What if everyone started doing this consciously? Let's start this movement. When women collectively intention something, the world changes. Can you envision a world of more love, positivity, and kindness? Gather with your like-minded women. Listen from your heart. Know that they have the wisdom to create a better world—and lend your energy where you can.

This chapter is an excerpt from my book about the journey to feminine power. If you love the principle **"When Women Gather, The World Changes"** you'll enjoy the *Feminine Power Cards* wisdom deck (FemininePowerCards.com) that inspired this chapter. Gather your girlfriends, play with these cards, and discuss the principles and practices. They will bring you new awareness and healing, emerge more of your authentic power, and create a better world for all. Let me know how it goes.

Laura Rubinstein, CHt, Social Buzz Club founder, is an award-winning digital media and marketing strategist, certified hypnotherapist, speaker, and author of the Feminine Power Cards and bestselling book Social Media Myths BUSTED. *Laura also serves on the Leadership Team for Women Speakers Association and hosts the* WSA-TV Premier Show. *Look for her upcoming book on feminine power.*

www.transformtoday.com

Pangs of Guilt

Anita D. Russell

"She's gone and I'm still here . . . how the world just carried on."
—*Michelle Obama*, Becoming

One hundred fifty-nine. Or 159. No matter how you write it, the number 159 is not a good number to hear when getting your blood pressure checked. I could easily lie to you and say that except for the blood pressure thing, this day was like any other for me as the part-time sibling bereavement coordinator at Children's Hospital of Pittsburgh (CHP). It certainly was not, however. In a matter of hours, that number went from 159 to 189. And I knew for sure something was wrong.

Grief. Guilt. Depression. I have experienced all three during different seasons of life, simultaneously tying together my past, present, and future. If my life were a library, there would be one shelf bookended with the death of my sister in 1962 and the death of my mom in 2017. On this particular shelf would be a book, *The Pangs of Guilt*, an in-depth analysis of my personal battle with managing guilt, especially when connected to grief.

In 1962, when Laney, my three-year-old sister, was killed, I witnessed the accident and spent the next several decades harboring guilt. That guilt was purely irrational, yet at the same time it became a part of my identity— so much so that I decided to go to medical school, become a pediatrician, and spend my career saving children from the perils of death. However, in an instant, the pathway to medical school gently closed in 1975. As I stood in line to register for my first year of classes at the Penn State Allegheny campus, God whispered into my spirit saying, *This is not what you're supposed to be doing.*

Fast-forward to 2017. While standing in the midst of trauma, watching my mother go through end-of-life issues, I made a guilt-ridden decision. My mom's illness brought me back to my home city of Pittsburgh, Pennsylvania, and I was ill-prepared for what was happening. When I heard "stage 4 metastasized breast cancer" within the context of *my* mom, I was perplexed. I discovered that my mom had been battling cancer of this magnitude since 2014—*for three years, and I had no idea*. My only thought—*What do we have to do to fight this?*—reflected denial so intense that its realization did not hit me until the morning of the day she passed away.

Grief over losing her coupled with the guilt of not knowing drove me to accept a part-time position as sibling bereavement coordinator in the Supportive Care Department of CHP. During the end-of-life process, including bereavement, the staff at Magee-Womens Hospital had supported my family. So I took this job assuming that I could help family members, siblings in particular, go through bereavement and thus honor my mom. In the interview, I shared my experiences with sibling loss and expressed the belief that I could be of help simply because I had been there. The interview was successful, and I was hired; I started one month after losing my mom.

This decision directly correlates with my decision to pursue a medical career as a pediatrician—both were based on deep-seated guilt. For years I pondered why God informed me that going to medical school was not part of my destiny. Prior to getting the CHP interview, I prayed for a part-time position—not for financial reasons but to ease my troubled mind. I prayed for a twenty-hour-per-week position where I could help someone going through the same storm as me. God, in His infinite grace, blessed me with exactly what I thought I wanted. It turns out His blessing was more instruction than provision.

Just like after Laney's death, guilt led to depression. Eventually depression settled into my body, manifesting itself in altered sleep patterns and feelings of dread deep within my gut. Those feelings of dread showed up whenever I got off the bus, as I walked across the driveway, and as I passed through the door into CHP space. In that space I relived the same conversations over and over again that I had heard as my mother's battle raged on— conversations about pain, medication, and dying; conversations layered on top of sorrow. Reading patient reports on cause of death—cancer, car accidents, gunshots, or suicide.

Around that same time, three things occurred in the background: the murder of a Pittsburgh teen by a police officer; the drive-by murder of a young college student; and a mass shooting in Trenton, New Jersey, where my daughter missed being there by about fifteen minutes. Everything came to a head when I heard the number 189.

Finally, it hit me—what God wanted me to see. Simply put, I am not built with the emotional stamina to deal with the daily suffering of children. I stopped watching the news regularly years ago after the 1994 murder of Megan Kanka. When the children at Sandy Hook were murdered, I cried as if they were my own. God knew, yet He allowed me to see for myself.

In 2019 I created a workbook, *6 Keys to Nurture, Grow and Empower Your Life*. The first key, Know Yourself, explains the importance of developing your strength areas while managing your weaknesses. My strength lies in my ability to connect with others, inspiring them to know themselves on a deeper level, and cultivating the change necessary to live their best life. I am truly blessed knowing that the work I do is meaningful and serves others purposefully, while allowing me to simultaneously nurture self-care.

This brings me to the CHP Supportive Care staff. They represent a dynamic group of professionals, destined for the job of helping patients, parents, families, and siblings deal with difficult issues such as end-of-life, grief, and bereavement. I am a better person having known them, and it is comforting to know that their emotional stamina for this work far outweighs my own.

Dedicated to the Supportive Care Staff
at Children's Hospital of Pittsburgh

Anita D. Russell is passionate about life coaching and doing BIG things—building community, inspiring change, and giving back. Anita is the founder of The Place to SOAR, a social enterprise engaged in cultivating daily growth and personal development. She is the author of I Wanna See Laney's House, a sibling story.

www.theplacetosoar.com

It's Never Too Early to Pursue Your Business: Hacks for Studentpreneurs

Alexis Schomer

One of the most critical things I learned as a "studentpreneur" was how to be extremely resourceful. If you combine drive and motivation with resourcefulness and critical thinking, nothing can stop you. Utilizing available resources is the key to moving forward on the journey to accomplish your goals. No matter where you are on your journey, believe that reaching your goal is possible and you can succeed. Whether you're a student or a seasoned executive, you can work on your mindset in order to optimize opportunities to your benefit.

As a student entrepreneur, you have many resources available. Don't let the moment get the best of you—don't tell yourself there's no way you can start a business while being a full-time student, working part-time, and maintaining a social life. The reality is that it is possible, and it actually is ideal. Being a student gives you more leverage than being in the workforce because of the resources available to you. For example, there are many student-only business competitions that provide non-dilutive funding, in-kind services, and many other prizes or incentives. As a student, you have access to professors with industry expertise who are essentially free consultants. You also have access to all of the free resources your university provides, such as printing, database access, survey software, sponsored tickets to events, and so on.

I started my first company during college, and I wish I had done it sooner. Yes, you will have to sacrifice some of your social life. Yes, you will have very long days. Yes, you will work in between classes. Yes, you will be thinking about your company nonstop. Yes, it is possible. And yes, it is worth it. Whether you're just starting out or you're almost at the end of your journey, one piece of advice that everyone can consume is "fail often and fail fast." The best learning experiences come from failure, and as an entrepreneur, you cannot be scared of failing. Take advantage of the opportunity to start working on your passion before the rest of the crowd. The earlier you start, the earlier you can fail, and the earlier you will succeed.

Another reason it's beneficial to start your company in college is that you don't have 100 percent of the responsibilities of a working professional. You're cut a lot of slack, get discounts, and generally don't have to worry about putting food on the table and supporting a family. Being a young entrepreneur has its perks; being younger, you can take more risks. Imagine if you decided to quit your job at forty years old with a family to support; the pressure is a lot higher, and you may not have the financial freedom to quit your existing job to start a business. Take advantage of having less responsibility and go for it.

It does not take a big investment to start building a company. In fact, I did it with almost no capital. Think of repurposing your current spending habits. For example, instead of spending $100 on coffee per month (or $100 on going out), invest that money in building your dreams and goals. Imagine what $100 could do if you put it toward a strategic plan to develop your business. You could pay for a website ($12/month), business cards ($50), and other beneficial items.

Growing up with technology has given today's young adults advantages over all of the generations before us. Technology is a core component of business and daily life. Generally speaking, millennials and generations proceeding are much more technically savvy than the preceding ones. Because of the importance and societal dependence on technology, we truly have an inside advantage.

When you're a student, your brain is like a sponge. You absorb information rapidly and quickly. This mindset is very powerful and can be used for business purposes as well as school. Absorb as much information as you can while you still think like a student.

You don't need to feel like you're alone in this process either. While driven young entrepreneurs are a rare breed, know that many before you, including myself, have paved the way for you—and it's a liberating path. Don't be scared; be excited! Reach out to mentors and entrepreneurs for advice. Get organized and strategically plan your milestones, which you can set monthly, daily, and weekly. You can turn your passion into a business with the right mindset. You can turn anything into a business if you're willing and able to pivot when necessary and learn from customer feedback. This is what's called the entrepreneurial mindset, and it can be learned. Shifting your mentality from identifying problems to seeing solutions is a game changer. Problems are just opportunities to create successful businesses around specific and purposeful solutions. This shift in mindset is the key to entrepreneurship and innovation.

Use this three-step challenge to help shift your mindset:

1. Write down every problem you think of, come across, or are frustrated by for an entire week.
2. Shortlist the top ten problems and think of solutions for each one.
3. Choose the one you feel most passionate about, and here you have an idea for a business. (Disclaimer: don't put money into this solution before you validate that customers would pay for it and it solves a real problem; make sure you learn more about validating your product and finding the right product/market fit).

I'll leave you with one last piece of advice: be open to change and do not become obsessed with your idea. It's likely that your vision may not be a perfect fit for the market, and you'll need to make some alterations to match market demand. Leave all bias at the door if you are truly passionate about what you're working on.

If you have an idea, passion, or curiosity for entrepreneurship, I encourage you to take the risk and start your journey today.

Alexis Schomer is a serial entrepreneur with a passion for solving problems through innovation. Born and raised in Los Angeles, she co-founded her first tech start-up while still in college. She is a frequent speaker at educational and motivational events, publishes, and is a consultant in addition to running her current company.

www.alexisschomer.com

LEARNING TO UNDERSTAND

MissyJena

"Where did I come from? Why am I here?" As a child, I was filled with a deep curiosity and desire to learn, especially about people. Looking back, understanding the role I was meant to play would be the greatest mystery. Yet the clues were always there—I only needed to learn how to decipher them.

As a child, I loved school . . . most of the time. There were other times no teacher could compete with my imagination. I had learned how to look as though I were paying attention while being completely tuned out (bouncing around the moon, exploring oceans, or thinking about things I had read in the news). Whenever I didn't understand why I had to learn something, I'd check out and happily be lost in my own world. I had a special knack for later figuring out how to complete assignments and projects. My grades, for the most part, were unaffected by my tendency to "tune out." That is, until I failed grade ten math. Sitting in summer school, I watched the teacher write out complicated math equations. I didn't get any of it. I felt like the dumbest kid in the world. Instead of writing down the equations, I wrote myself a note: "I will dedicate my life to children and make sure no other child feels the way I do right now."

Over the thirty-two years I spent in schools, both as a student and an educator, I never stopped wondering . . .

Why are there some children in the world *who would do anything to* be able to go school, while other children *would do anything to not have* to go to school? At what point did our well-intentioned goals of educating children turn into something children resist and reject?

In September 2001 I started working in a school as an "Urgent Interventionist." I was filled with excitement and ambition on the first day. The next day the world had changed. We struggled to come to terms with the devastation and destruction of 9/11. It was a shocking start to a new chapter in life. I profoundly understood I was now a responsible part of the ecosystem within schools—which affects what happens in the world outside. I held this responsibility as a complex honor and special mission to navigate. Tuned in, I began to pay close attention to the process of learning. I was curious to discover what genuinely caused children to light up. What made them shut down?

It took me fifteen years of closely observing the learning process and subtle nuances in communication to recognize the gaps that were occurring in schools. I began testing "calmversation" as a new model for learning with the following questions guiding my intentions.

What if we provided students with the tools, skills, and creative learning opportunities to champion each child exactly where they are intellectually, socially, or emotionally? What if we could reduce their stress and anxiety while boosting their potential to learn, lead and inspire? What if classrooms became an exciting hub of joy, creativity and compassion?

I was on to something, and everyone around me knew it. . . . Students who were previously disengaged were actively involved and excited to learn. We were taking the "con" out of conversation and bringing calmversation to life. Curiosity, laughter, authentic dialogues, and genuine smiles were occurring inside of classrooms and spilling out into the hallways and playgrounds.

In 2015 I was faced with a dilemma. Do I leave the comfort and security of the schools I'd known, or do I take what I have learned and make calmversation available for the benefit of more children? It would be safe to stay and scary to leave. The path before me was filled with uncertainty. There was no one to show me how to do this. The day I built up the courage to hand in my resignation, I was elated and terrified. My principal at the time, a true leader, held my hand and nudged me out the door. "Jena, I need you, but the world needs you more," and with those words I was released.

By spring 2016 the calmversation curriculum was ready for testing. Feedback from the children and educators who participated was better than I could have predicted. Children felt understood, valued, and respected, and they were excited to learn from each other. As I visited each of the participating classrooms, key questions began to emerge. "How did you know we needed this? Who taught you how to make this program?"

The children have always been my greatest teachers and in answering their questions, the mysteries of my own life started to unravel. It was time to take the risk to share rather than keep it safe and secure within my own reach.

Later that year, I stepped onto the TEDxSFU stage to talk about "Taking the Leap for Education." It was a sold-out theatre with the biggest audience I'd ever stood before. I looked into the crowd and saw the ones who most deeply understood the risk I took. My parents, friends, family and why even my doctor appeared to make some noise. In their presence and unwavering belief, I delivered the "4 Truths" which summarizes what I have learned about educating children:

1. You can't force someone to learn.
2. Nor can you demand attention and expect to sustain it.
3. A child that has not known respect has none to spare.
4. The child's brain belongs to the child.

I held a key to the complex puzzle of making education relevant and more meaningful for children. Years later, I marvel at the impact calmversation has had because of the sparkling humans who stepped forward to make this cause a reality for children.

I invite you to reflect on your own experiences as a child and imagine what would have happened if you had a structure to positively support your own growth and development. As one student declared, "A calmversation is a time to relax with your brain and understand things better."

Take a moment to reflect on your own experiences as a child. All the wishes and wisdoms you've collected hold important clues about who you are and why you are here. Now imagine if you had a structure for learning that magnified your inner gifts and brilliance?

From my heart to yours, let's keep the calmversation going . . .

Jena Sharma, better known as "MissyJena" is the kindest troublemaker you'll ever meet! She is an educator, innovator, and professional speaker who has developed a unique system to dissolve barriers to learning and communication. Her desire to make a difference led her to establish **calmversation**™, *a multidimensional approach to authentic, creative, and high-impact communication.*

www.calmversation.org

Finding Courage in Your Story

Terry Sidford

It was 1970 and I was living in Encinitas, California. I was eight years old. My sister and I were in our bedroom when suddenly she blurted out, "Terry, grab whatever you can—we have to leave tonight."

"*What?* Tonight? Why?"

"Mom and Jerry have never been this drunk, and something might happen to us."

Frightened and confused, I grabbed a pillowcase and put whatever clothes were on the floor inside. "Debi, I can't leave my goldfish. Can we take them with us?"

"No, Terry, we have to walk to Dad's house *now*."

We ran out of our apartment in the dark toward my father's apartment. My sister had called him and told him we were coming, and he ran out to find us. As we walked across the railroad tracks, I remember feeling like a homeless person escaping something dangerous. My father found us and took us to his bachelor pad. We never lived with our mother again.

My father was a counselor at the community college. He was loving and kind, but he was a free spirit, to say the least. He did his best to cook us healthy meals—mainly tuna casseroles and lentil soups.

I was the youngest of three children. My sister left home right after high school, and my brother (who had also eventually moved in with our dad) graduated early. I was the only one left at home when my father's girlfriend moved in.

When I was in high school, my father's girlfriend and I didn't get along. I was unhappy and insecure. Not only did I have an alcoholic mother, but now I was unhappy at home living what seemed to be an unstable life with my father. I left high school my junior year to live with my sister in Arizona.

My self-esteem was so low that I couldn't bring myself to enroll in another high school there. I decided to get a job and work instead.

Years later I obtained a GED, which is equivalent to a high school diploma. I should have been proud, but I still felt ashamed for not finishing high school.

Having an alcoholic mother who couldn't care for me and being a high school dropout only added to all my other insecurities. To compensate, my outward appearance became more polished so no one could see the pain on the inside.

In my twenties, I worked in the medical field, becoming an angiographer and surgical assistant. During this time, I met my first husband. He was kind, stable, and reliable. We had two beautiful children, Alex and Connor. Eventually, though, I became restless. I felt I was living an inauthentic life that kept me from expressing my true feelings and emotions. My husband liked that I worked full-time because of the income, but he also wanted me to be a full-time mother. I tried to tell him it was impossible to be a perfect mother and still work full-time, but he wouldn't listen.

Finally, through much soul-searching, I faced my fears and doubts about making it on my own. I believed in something inside of me that said: "You will be all right; trust this voice." After that, I bravely gave myself permission to pursue my dream of becoming a pharmaceutical representative, even though I did not have a college degree. I wanted this job so badly that I applied for it with nothing more than faith in myself. And you know what? I got it!

This gave me the confidence and courage I needed to make the tough decision to initiate a divorce. It was hard because I knew I would get tremendous disapproval from everyone around me. But I found strength I never knew I had. It took courage and heart to know that my two sweet sons would be better off with a mother who was whole rather than one who was broken. It was as if a force deep inside me knew I had no other choice but to live my truth, and that truth would sustain me.

This was my first step in finding my courage. At that moment I changed my life story from one of being insecure and ashamed to one of infinite possibilities.

As the years went on, I remarried and started a career in life coaching that led me to work with women. I found it curious that many women were incredibly brave, but they never saw it in themselves. I wanted to find out why. I created a survey on courage and found one hundred women willing to take it. I compiled my findings into stories, each illustrating a different aspect of a woman's courage. When I finished, the stories became my book *100 Hearts: Inspiring Stories from the Women Who Lived Them.*

One evening I gave a presentation at a women's book club, and one of the ladies asked for examples of my own courage. I was completely taken aback. *My own courage? What do I say?* I answered weakly, "I find courage in my day-to-day life." I went home and thought about it. I knew it had taken courage for me to get a divorce; it took courage to pursue a new career. Yet I still felt ashamed of what had happened in my life. But when I thought about how I had survived the dark times in my life, I realized that my ability to survive pain, abandonment, humiliation, and self-doubt from my past took tremendous courage. Overcoming shame and embarrassment took a huge amount of courage too. That night I reaffirmed my choice to make the shift from "I am ashamed and embarrassed" to "I find my strength and courage in my stories."

You deserve to be seen, heard, loved, and valued regardless of your life story. Acknowledging the courage that results from your life stories allows you to be seen and heard for who you are today. And being honest and open about yourself paves the way for others around you to do the same.

Terry Sidford is a motivational TEDx speaker, author, professional coach, and television host who transforms audiences through sharing her life experiences of embarrassment, past failures, and triumphs. Terry inspires audiences to write new, courageous chapters of their own life stories. She and her family live in beautiful Park City, Utah.

www.terrysidford.com

Unleashing My Voice

Carma Spence

"Your templates are wrong!"

My opinions about the movie we just saw were wrong. My way of finding a job was wrong. My sorrow at the loss of my dog of fourteen years was wrong. It didn't matter what I said, did, or felt, my husband always said that my templates were wrong.

After three years of this, I contemplated divorce. However, I gave it another ten years—just in case things would get better.

By the time I walked away from that marriage, I could barely recognize myself. I had spent more than a decade packing away bits and pieces of who I was into a hiding place deep within me, silencing my unique voice.

I moved from Arizona to California to start a new life. However, it wasn't new enough. *I* had not changed.

***

When I was three, my family moved to East Africa, where I attended preschool. The year I turned five, my little sister was born disabled and we moved back to the States to give her access to better healthcare. My parents became absorbed in her care, and I had to be a "big girl."

The message I took away from this experience was that I didn't matter, and so I became very shy and introverted. I began to silence my voice.

I was bullied in school. I withdrew even more.

When I was a junior in high school and my speech teacher asked me to join the speech team, I was shocked. But I did it anyway. Little did I know that this would be a critical component to unleashing my voice later in life.

***

After I left my husband and moved to California, I got into another relationship that was even worse. One night, after casually mentioning that I liked the president, my boyfriend flew into a rage and stormed off to get drunk. He returned late that night and attacked me. He poured a bottle of water on me as I was sleeping in bed. He choked me. He called me a traitor to my country and said I deserved to be lined up against a wall and shot. He took my phone and hid it. He slapped me in the face, resulting in a fractured orbital (the bone that holds your eye in place). Later, I heard him laughing on the phone with his brother, telling him that he had "waterboarded" his girlfriend.

When he finally fell asleep, I got dressed, grabbed my laptop, and fled my apartment. I was terrified and didn't know what to do. I ended up in a McDonald's where I chatted with a friend over Skype about what was going on. She convinced me to call the police. I borrowed a phone from one of the clerks. The cops took my boyfriend away, and within months he was sentenced to four years in prison.

That's when I realized, "If I don't get my act together, the next guy will kill me."

I spent the next year working on myself. I stopped dating, and I dedicated myself to improving my confidence and sense of self-worth.

I attended domestic violence prevention classes. I worked with a therapist. I studied Universal Laws. I covered my apartment with sticky notes on which I had written positive statements and affirmations. I dove into Toastmasters, exploring different ways to speak my truth. Over time, I slowly but surely released my voice from its prison within me. But my journey wasn't over.

In April 2015, I went on a date with a different kind of man. I was determined to be "all out Carma," and if he didn't like it, I would walk.

He loved it!

We became fast friends, spending hours and hours talking about life, faith, and superheroes. We became inseparable. I lost count of how many times strangers asked us, "How long have you been married?"

In August 2015—on my birthday—he took me to Disneyland and proposed to me by Snow White's Wishing Well. After a startled, "Seriously? Seriously? Really? Seriously?" I answered, "Yes!"

In February 2016, just a couple days after confirming all the members of our wedding party, I was struck by a car while crossing the street. I flew several feet into the air and broke my nose. My skull was fractured in multiple places, as were my ribs, hips, and left arm. I lost two of my front teeth. More than one doctor commented to me that he was surprised I was alive and not brain-damaged.

As part of my healing process, while laid up in the hospital and then in a rehabilitation center learning to walk again, I shared my recovery journey on Facebook. I was surprised and deeply moved by the outpouring of love I received. Strangers and people I barely knew sent me flowers!

But the response that touched me the most was when the teenaged son of a high school acquaintance was so inspired by my posts that he decided to pursue his dreams. That's when I knew that simply by being me, I made a difference in the world.

In October 2016, I was able to dance with my new husband at our wedding reception.

***

Today, I'm an award-winning author, editor, and speaker. I've been featured in an international bestseller. And, most importantly, I'm comfortable in my own skin—no matter how imperfect it may be.

None of this would have happened if I had not unleashed my voice. My templates were not wrong after all!

Carma Spence, speaker and author of the award-winning bestseller Public Speaking Super Powers, *is fiercely committed to helping women, introverts, and shy people unleash their inner content creation superhero and communicate their message with confidence so they can create a meaningful legacy.*

www.publicspeakingsuperpowers.com

BECOMING THE WOMAN OF MY GRANDMOTHER'S DREAMS

Allison K. Summers

I reached down and ran my hand across the package I had stowed under the seat in front of me. The plane hadn't even pulled away from the gate, and I was nervously making sure it was right where I had placed it. I had grown accustomed to the routine of overnight flights and my predictable window seat on the sunrise side of the plane. Typically, one could find me settled in with all the essentials critical to make a tiny economy seat my home away from home: my kids' pictures tucked in my Bible, fluffy sleep socks, pillows, and an abundance of chocolate to serve as a proper antidote for stress from turbulence or annoying travel companions. But this flight was different. This time I was carrying an irreplaceable item that had belonged to my grandmother—her 1920's art deco scrapbook lovingly filled with seventy years of dreams—and this scrapbook had a place that it needed to go.

Born in 1910, the world was limited for my grandmother, but in her own way she knew how to grab hold of the simplest things and make magic. When she was twelve, the tomb of King Tut was discovered, and this ignited a lifelong passion of acquiring books on pyramids, wearing Egyptian jewelry, sewing fabric hieroglyphics, clipping articles, drawing sketches, and weaving unbelievable stories for her grandchildren about archeology and mummies. For decades she added to her collection, and then one day, she gave her overstuffed, worn-out scrapbook to me. She said it was mine because she knew I would take the best care of it.

At the time, I didn't make as much of it as I should have, and I regret that. My grandmother's life wasn't easy, nor was my mother's—nor honestly was mine for many years. Growing up, I didn't know women even had the option of pursuing a professional career; after all, it's tough to be what you can't see. My home was a battlefield where money was usually scarce and religious wars raged on, but through my grandmother I learned to envision far-off places and a world beyond where I stood.

I was fortunate and made it to college. There I thought I had met a prince, but that relationship only introduced me to the cycle of abuse, a tough escape, and hard lessons learned. But along the way, an odd thing happened: I fell into business and discovered I was good at it.

At first, I was naïve. I didn't care about a career path; I only knew that I needed more money in my pocket because money meant freedom— something the women in my family had always lacked. Wisely, I had determined that observation was key. What were those men who had the window offices doing? How did you get into the inner circle? Through perseverance, I mastered the art of gaining knowledge I lacked. One day the vice president walked through the office looking for someone with a passport to hand-carry a package to London that very day. *Opportunity,* I thought. So, the next week I applied for a passport and set an intention to see the world.

Fast-forward through job titles and years; I had eventually worked "heels on the ground" in thirty countries. Then in 2013 came the trip with the precious scrapbook.

While serving as the executive director of an international travel association, I was finally heading to the land of my grandmother's dreams, Egypt, to speak at a tourism summit. But travel was not without concern in the post-revolution era. After months of protests, conflicts, travel warnings, embassy closures, and the nightly news media blasting images of dissidence from Tahrir Square, my family wasn't pleased that I was making such a trip. It's unnecessary, they said; you have kids to worry about. And it was true; I had three children at home and a marriage that drained me. It wasn't clear to anyone else why I needed to get on that plane, but I couldn't ignore the spirit of my grandmother, and I wanted with all my heart to leverage what I had achieved in my career to honor her.

Cairo was strange at that time—it was certainly filled with tension, yet the people held an optimism not conveyed in the media. At a quick glance, the burned-out National Democratic Party's headquarters seemed to cast a dark shadow over the Egyptian National Museum, but the locals pointed proudly to the building and touted hopes for a better economic future. Our guides took us throughout the region, which including climbing inside the Great Pyramid. As exciting as those things were, for me the main event belonged to my grandmother.

The travel summit ballroom buzzed with excitement and gratitude at our arrival. I stepped on the stage, hugging my grandmother's book; before me sat the minister of tourism and my association president. I looked at them, smiled, and told the crowd the love story of my grandmother and her Egyptian dreams. I opened the scrapbook and gently held up faded articles and yellowed fabrics. When I looked at the two men again, they had tears in their eyes. Later the minister threw his arms around me in appreciation as if I had saved a country, and my president scolded me for causing him to tear up in public.

As I packed to return to Chicago, I stared at the Nile from the hotel room window and wondered, *Would I have been able to break free and lead my own life if my grandmother had not taught me to dream beyond my circumstances?* I wondered what I would pass on in my own life legacy, and then I cried as I thought about my children and how much I missed them.

I always say that people who achieve more in life dare to see beyond the space they currently occupy. I hope that you, too, *may see the world beyond your today—and then set intentions and actions to take you there.*

Allison K. Summers is a global leader and recognized champion of women in business. She is the author of Connect to Influence, *the host of Disruptive CEO Nation, and a frequent guest on radio, TV, and event platforms. Her passion is coaching and training business professionals to achieve their fullest human potential.*

www.AllisonKSummers.com

What Doesn't Kill You Makes You Stronger

Susan Thomas

I was born in Los Angeles and grew up in a poor area of Southern California. Our family of five lived in a tiny, two-bedroom house in Los Alamitos, which we rented until I attended high school. My sister and I shared a bunk bed, and my brother slept on a trundle bed that he pulled out each night. My mom was the only breadwinner, which in the sixties was unheard of. She worked at the same company for over forty years.

My father was an alcoholic and never kept a job for long. I still remember the collection calls. The ignoring the phone or me answering the phone to tell them my dad was not home, when he was. Not an ideal childhood.

I still remember when I was in eighth grade and my mom told us we didn't have enough money to buy all three kids back-to-school clothes. I told my mom to take care of the younger two first. I felt it was my duty as the oldest sibling to help my mom, as I knew it made her very sad not to provide for us the way she wanted to. She did manage to get me two pairs of pants, one pair of white pants and one brown pair. Later that year I got a pair of jeans with some cute bunnies on it. But I soon realized that only having three pairs, I should have gone with the plain jeans. With a limited supply of clothes, the other kids noticed as I had to wear them more than one time per week.

When I was seventeen, we moved into a resort-style trailer park. It had lots of amenities—a pool, tennis courts, a restaurant and a pub, a corner store, and a game room. Soon after I met the man who would become my husband. We both attended college and worked in a clothing store to pay for our education. Scholarships were a foreign concept to us, and neither set of parents could afford to send any of their children to university. I studied to become a nurse practitioner, and my fiancé took printing courses. We could sit in on any class, so I hung out with him in his classes. I found biology courses very hard, so I started paying attention to his printing courses and found them much easier to understand. My soon-to-be husband shared his dream of starting his own printing company. We soon found that the things he excelled at, I didn't, but in the areas he didn't, I excelled. We were a perfect team.

When I was nineteen, my fiancé's dad's visa was about to expire, and his family returned to Canada. My husband asked me to go too, and we got married soon after before a Justice of the Peace.

I found out immediately that my future mother-in-law was verbally and emotionally abusive toward me; I sensed a deep hatred from her.

Within a short time of arriving in Canada, I found out I was pregnant. My fiancé was worried that it would ruin our lives, and I was pressured into having an abortion. I immediately regretted it and went into a depression. I am now pro-choice, but until my daughter was born years later, I didn't understand the reality of a baby growing inside me.

After I got my landed immigrant status, my husband and I both worked very hard, and with a loan from each of our parents of a thousand dollars each, we started our company, a small manufacturing company in Surrey, BC. In 1985, I found out I was pregnant, and I gave birth to a beautiful baby girl. The doctors noticed right away she had bilateral club feet, a rare birth defect that would affect her height. She had numerous surgeries, and she still has chronic pain every day. She is now in her early thirties, and I have two wonderful grandkids.

During the nineties, our company won many prestigious awards, and I held many board positions and was very active in the community. In 2011 I ran for Surrey City Council. Unfortunately, I was not successful, but I met a lot of people and learned a lot from the experience. We eventually sold our business after thirty years, and I realized that I am an entrepreneur. I took some time to figure out what I wanted to do with the next chapter in my life, and then I started a business, Premier Coaching & Consulting. My signature program is "The Passion-Driven Purpose." I realized that my passion was helping other people discover their passion, and my favorite part is when they have an aha moment.

During this time, we dealt with a few family matters. In 2015 my daughter left her abusive husband, and she and her kids now live with us. The kids have been dealing with PTSD, abandonment, and more.

My youngest grandchild came out as transgender from the time he was three and a half years old and has been diagnosed with gender dysphoria. I believe Caitlyn Jenner coming out really helped, as it was at the same time. Then in 2019 a close family member was raped by someone she thought was a friend.

From the outside looking in, my life might look easy to others. My experiences have been hard to deal with, but I always have found a way to become more empowered, wiser, and stronger. Each life lesson can be looked at as either a failure or a life lesson learned. I choose to learn from every experience.

Remember to mentor the younger generation, give back to your community, and appreciate what you have. You can make the changes to move forward; it is up to you. You live life only once, so choose wisely on how you react to what life throws at you. I have had to work hard for everything in my life, but I can say with confidence that when you earn it, you appreciate it more.

Susan Thomas is a well-respected certified business coach, entrepreneur, and motivational speaker. She has received industry recognition for her outstanding achievements and leadership. A strong advocate, volunteer, and community supporter, Susan's passion is helping others discover their passion, find their purpose, and achieve their goals.

www.premiercoaching.ca

MONKEY BARS

Francine Tone

"Happiness is not something ready-made.
It comes from your own actions." —*Dalai Lama*

It's a hot, humid summer afternoon in Japan, with mosquitos buzzing and the smell of DDT lingering in the air. My family lives on a military base. I'm five years old and playing outside with three of my friends. Suddenly, my three friends circle me, yelling repeatedly, "Your mother is dead!"

I start crying. I run home, into the kitchen where my mother is fixing dinner. She asks, "What's the matter?"

I reply through my tears, "They're saying you're dead!"

That evening, my parents sat me down and explained that my friends were right. My Japanese mother was dead. She died when I was a year old, and my American father left me with my Japanese grandmother. The couple who I thought were my parents had adopted me when I was five.

My adoptive father spent considerable time telling me how special I was because he and my adoptive mother had chosen me. I went to bed that night feeling reassured and loved.

A few weeks later, I learned how special I really was. I had gone to bed, with the lights out and the door closed. My adoptive father quietly entered my room. He began touching me in ways I did not understand. That was the start of my new reality until I was twenty years old. On any given night, for those fifteen years, I did not know what was in store for me.

But daytime was my time. I would leave the house and go to the playground. There, I chose to focus my attention on being the best at the monkey bars—better than the boys. I learned to hang from the bars, move from bar to bar, and swing anywhere I wanted. I became an expert on the monkey bars. When I was on the monkey bars, I didn't think about what had happened the night before. I just focused on the monkey bars and how and where I was swinging. I persevered to accomplish any new trick I set out to master. I did not think about what might happen to me that night. I stayed on the monkey bars all day, every day. Physically, mentally, and emotionally, the monkey bars and my skill on them consumed me. It was my way of taking action.

As I grew, I shifted my focus to different goals and tasks. I became an overachiever and sought out to master anything and everything with gusto. My perseverance often resulted in me winning awards if one was being offered. I was tenacious in everything I did. As I grew older, I refused to be a victim of what was happening to me, and I kept those moments segregated in a little bubble in my mind. I kept choosing action after action when the time was mine to control.

Of course, I picked up lots and lots of baggage along the way. During my teenage years, I would lie awake at night wishing I could change my life, often even wishing to end it. What kept me going was knowing that when my adoptive father was not having his way with me, I could control what I did. I had the power to take actions that impacted my life. I could become the best at the monkey bars. I could join a swim team and win ribbons and medals. I could work hard in school and get the highest grades. I could smile and laugh. I could set goals and achieve them.

Action propelled me to move forward and upward. I became an attorney, a business strategist, a speaker. I became a fully certified ski instructor, a dive master, a podium-finishing stand-up paddleboard racer, and surfer.

No matter what anyone else does to you or does around you, in the end you have the power to decide what you will do today. You have the power to decide what happens next in your life. There are times when you might feel you have no choice at all. Sometimes the choices you have are difficult. But knowing that action is yours for the taking keeps your mind always looking for opportunities. There you will find the choices. There, every day, you will find some action that will make a difference. Each day, there is a future you can mold based on opportunities you see, your choices, your decisions, and your actions.

One day, my adoptive father called and asked me to forgive him. I said yes, even though I didn't mean it. When he passed, initially I was angry that I could not retract the forgiveness. But I relied on my history of taking action and moved on to my next monkey bar.

Spending life energy wishing the past did not happen does nothing. Spending life energy wishing your past was different does not change anything. Spending life energy telling yourself and others that you are "victim" does not help. Your past is what it is, as was mine.

We are made up of a stack of rocks built over the course of our lives. Some rocks are flat and solid. Others are round and wobbly. Yet all the rocks stack neatly together. You cannot remove any and still be you.

Recognizing that the stack of rocks has made me who I am today may be the most important idea that has moved me forward and upward in life. If you have a lot of wobbly rocks, be grateful. Maybe it means you are stronger than the average. You have the strength within to make a choice and take an action—one small action that will make a difference in your life today. Each day, make a choice and take another action.

Just start. Pick something and do it. Do not wait for motivation or the right time. All you need to do is take one small step. Hang from a monkey bar. Sometimes, from the smallest action comes the biggest reward.

Francine Tone is a performance optimizer and living proof that stressed-out professionals can shift into a life of freedom by knowing which actions make the difference. An attorney, business strategist, speaker, three-time number-one bestselling author, and high-performance athlete, Francine lives with her husband/law partner Jeff in the mountains near Lake Tahoe, California.

www.FrancineTone.com

In This Gig Economy, It's Never Too Late: Reinvention at Sixty!

Lorianne Vaughan Speaks

Let me start by saying that I have had many careers over my lifetime. I was a political campaign worker and manager in my twenties, a headhunter (recruiter) in my thirties and forties, and then in my fifties, an office manager for a thought-leader with a multimillion-dollar business.

This thought-leader offered workshops to Fortune 1000 companies based on her best-selling books. After working fifteen years for her, I found myself laid off at the age of sixty when she sold her company. There I was, sending out resumes and not hearing one word back. What was I going to do? Corporate America did not want to hire a sixty-year-old!

Silly them!

I had a skill set that I knew could be used by many speakers and authors. My superpower has always been my organizational skills and ability to get things done. But how was I to get that skill set out to the masses? After much trial and error, I came to the conclusion that I needed to start and build my own virtual assistance company. **So I did!** And you know what? I learned I had even more superpowers, such as using social media (who knew!) and being a partner to help others grow and be more successful—and I learned that I love doing this!

Now, two years later, I have many clients, and I have hired other marginalized women with various skill sets that they use to help my clients grow their presence in social media, as well their time on the stage. My team and I partner with them to grow their businesses.

In 2019, according to data from the U.S. Labor Department, about 35 percent of the U.S. workforce *is employed on a contract basis*, and only 51 percent of workers are actually full-time employees within a company!

Times are changing—and it's time for us to start looking at our superpower skill sets and start using them to either supplement our regular income or build a business as I have.

I always wanted to be in business for myself. While raising my kids (as a single mom), I had four jobs at one point, and I was always selling something to supplement my income. I actually went out on my own as a recruiter when I wanted to work from home when the kids were little (and I still had my husband's income as a safety net). Then, after 9/11 when the market dried up and I needed to get a more stable job with regular income, I started my office manager role—but I never lost my entrepreneurial spirit.

Now my kids are all adults and settled in their own families, so when I found myself unemployed, I knew it was time to start my own company again—and do what I love doing: helping others be their best!

What do you do best? Identify your own superpowers and share them with the world!

If you are looking to venture out on your own, consider doing the following things now:

- Really look at yourself—what superpowers do you have to offer others? It could be writing, or graphic design, or the ability to speak and motivate others with your story.
- Get on *all* the social media platforms and make connections. The more you network, the more bandwidth you will have to spread your message.
- Follow that icon you want to be like and comment on their posts; you will be noticed by them and their followers, and they will see that you know your stuff (just make sure you are authentic).
- Tell people (but not necessarily your boss) about your plan. As you articulate your dream to others, you will better envision the plan and drill down to the specific skills or services you want to offer—and your friends can hold you accountable.
- Start small—you don't need to spend large amounts of money on every technical software and system to start. Begin with a small project, do it well, and then ask for referrals.

Everyone has an idea they want to grow—**just do it!**

No matter what your age, ethnicity, or physical capabilities, you, too, have superpowers! You can run a business from your home office and earn your desired income as you help others earn *their* desired income—whether as a supplement to your current income or an entity to take you to a new level of success.

You don't have to retire because you've reached a certain age, and you certainly don't need to give up! You can offer your skills on a project-by-project basis in this gig economy.

I am having a blast, and I'm meeting amazing people I never would have if that "scary" layoff had never happened! It's never too late to reinvent yourself and work your superpowers full-time or gig-by-gig!

Just do it!

Lorianne Vaughan Speaks, founder of LVS Consulting Services, assists authors, speakers, and podcasters to get their message out to the world (in both verbal and written form). Lorianne often speaks about how to find, work, and train virtual assistants for small companies, as well as share her inspiring story.

www.LVSConsultingServices.com

OLD DOG, NEW TRICKS

Dee Dee Vicino

When C.S. Lewis said, "You are never too old to set another goal or to dream a new dream," I wasn't listening. I was packing. Setting new goals and dreaming new dreams was so out of the realm of possibility for me, even if C.S. Lewis himself had sat me down and shaken his finger in my face, I would not have heard him. His words would have been unintelligible, his message lost in the mire of my reality.

In 2015 my only goal was to GET OUT. Get out of South Florida. Get my child out of danger. The only dream I was dreaming was one of peace—living in a world in which the police weren't calling about my daughter or pounding on my door in the middle of the night to inform me that she had been involved in a car accident. A world in which my neighbors weren't calling to tell me she was sneaking out of the house in the middle of the night (again). A world in which drugs, neatly packaged in water bottles, weren't tucked into the foliage surrounding my home. A world in which her "friends" were not breaking into my home, stealing her things, or threatening her life. A world devoid of juvenile court, community service, and restraining orders. That was the dream I was dreaming. That was the life I was fleeing.

And flee I did—to colorful Colorado. There I gave myself permission to rest. To heal. To put the past behind us and focus on the future. Both of my children flourished in Colorado. My oldest daughter continued to pursue her college studies and enjoy college life. My youngest *thrived*. Removed from familiar surroundings and sketchy acquaintances, she took time to reacquaint herself with herself. She meditated. She journaled. She enrolled in the local community college and began her college studies while completing an online high school program. Two years flew by, and with both children happy and healthy and self-sufficient, it was time for Mom to get a job.

The hunt began. The incredibly. Frustrating. Hunt. A former English teacher and assistant principal who was forty-nine years young, I focused on the education industry. While I found *plenty* of jobs (and even went on a few interviews), I couldn't seem to land a job. I later discovered that the jobs for which I interviewed went to those already working in the school district—and much younger too. *Every. Single. Time.* This continued for about a year. I learned something very important during that year: I needed to change industries.

But if I wasn't a teacher or an administrator, who was I? C.S. Lewis spoke again, and this time I listened. The school system may have deemed me too old, but C.S Lewis assured me that I was not too old to dream a new dream, and certainly not too old to set a new goal. It was time for this old dog—now fifty—to learn a few new tricks.

The first new trick involved revisiting old tricks. What *could* I do? What did I *want* to do? What did I *love* to do? What skills did I possess? Once I answered these questions, I expanded my job search and targeted a new industry. I reinvented myself, rebranded myself. And it *worked*. In less than a month, I found my "dream job"—director of training and education for one of the largest food-allergy training companies in the country.

During the initial interview, it was clear that I lacked experience with commercial kitchens (completely foreign to me) and with the e-learning world (only mildly foreign to me). Yep, this old dog needed to learn a second trick. This trick involved gaining experience in the areas where there was lack, post haste. I quickly made arrangements to tour several commercial kitchens so I had an understanding of how restaurants accommodated customers with food allergies and intolerances. I took that knowledge and created a training program using an innovative e-learning platform I found online. After a few follow-up emails and a lunch meeting, I got the job.

This is the part where I jump up and down and cry tears of joy and post my success all over social media, right? And I did . . . until I didn't. A disturbing realization displaced my short-lived enthusiasm: my dream job did not come with a dream boss. My boss was the embodiment of my former in-laws—those uber-traditional, quick-tempered New York Italians who hated that their only son had married an independent-thinking WASP. The ones I divorced along with that only son many moons ago. Enter trick number three: it's OK to walk away.

I walked right out of those oppressive offices and into a new life. A life in which I was in control. A life that I wanted to live. A life in which I made the calls. I threw caution to the wind and started my own business—one focused upon improving the lives of those with food allergies and other special dietary needs—and three new tricks was all it took:

1. Focus on what you CAN do, not what you CAN'T do.
2. Knowledge is power, and you CAN reclaim your power with knowledge.
3. Walk away from misery. Life is too short to remain in a job you don't like, in a relationship that isn't working, or in a questionable lifestyle.

When I fled Florida four years ago, I would never have dreamt that I would own my own business, speak at global medical summits and conferences on behalf of those with food allergies, or have a boutique cookbook on the shelf and others in the works. I certainly wouldn't have imagined that I would be a contributing author to an international bestselling book. So many undreamt dreams have come true for me. Thank you, C.S. Lewis, for reminding me that we are never too old to set new goals, dream new dreams, or learn new tricks!

Dee Dee Vicino is a recovering assistant principal who is passionate about increasing food allergy awareness in the U.S. and abroad. She ditched conventional wisdom when she left her dream job and launched her own business. Today, she speaks on an international stage providing inspiration for food allergy sufferers everywhere.

www.allercuisine.com

YOUR LIFE CAN LIGHT THE WAY

Elaine Voci, PhD

What are you passionate about? In how many areas of your life does your passion play a role? Are you living the life that you've been called to live? I consider it a blessing that my passion, values, and lifelong aspirations have been shaped by the sacrifices of my Italian immigrant grandparents who came to America at the turn of the century.

In the shelter of their hopes and dreams, they had the courage to imagine a new life in the face of prejudice, the character to resist the worst of the culture around them, and the generosity of spirit to give the best of themselves. Armed with a willingness to work hard, the perseverance to keep pressing forward, and a resolute faith in themselves and in the goodness of others, they became respected members of their communities, and their lives burned brightly. To their offspring, they repeatedly emphasized their belief that education was the key to a fulfilling life because it would develop character and values such as kindness, bravery, honesty, and integrity.

From the time I entered school, I loved learning. I seemed destined to absorb their advice deeply. When I began an evening school program at a local college, I was already married with two toddlers at home. It took six years to complete my undergraduate degree, with honors, in spite of my husband's lukewarm support. I was awarded a teaching fellowship, and I went on to earn a master's degree. A few years later, I became the first person in my family to graduate with a doctoral degree—and also the first grandchild to be divorced.

As my life's work evolved, so did my sense of adventure. It compelled me to figure out how life works, to understand the role of intuition, and to trust in the Universe as a collaborative and friendly partner. It seemed to me that life gave me opportunities that were tailor-made for my growth. That process then encouraged me to dream with an open heart, hone my unique talents, and apply them in a world that longed for peace and unity.

When my youngest son began law school, I made an intentional choice to work abroad in order to feel at home in the larger world. The universe orchestrated a series of miraculous coincidences that placed me in Japan where I worked for four years, advancing my vocational skills and becoming a citizen diplomat.

I learned what it meant to be an American as I saw myself through the eyes of thousands of Japanese people, including coworkers, bosses, neighbors, and shop owners. When I came home to Indiana, I saw myself again, this time through American eyes. I was surprised to discover that I had unexpectedly joined a special club of people called "expatriates." These adventurers were curious about the world and proud to make friends across the cultural divide. They were storytellers whose tales always seemed to convey humor, humility, and a moral lesson.

I felt close to my Italian ancestors when I realized that they had been "expats" too. I understood for the first time why "Nickie the Baker" came to *both* of my grandparent's homes every week with huge loaves of fresh Italian bread, and why the same music and customs were always a part of the holidays on both sides of my family. I saw how natural it was for each couple to want to bring their siblings from the old country so that they, too, could find a new life in America.

I had so much in common with my grandparents: their lives, burning so brightly, had illuminated my life path, helped me to have the courage to navigate the world at large, and empowered me to meet the challenges of living abroad in order to grow. These experiences made me a better person, one with a deeper sense of gratitude and appreciation of so many things—my family's roots, my faith in people, my ability to survive and prosper, and my understanding that kindness and love are central to feeling accomplished as a human being.

As a life coach, I have used these stories to inspire clients, empower them, and show them that adventures of the heart are what make for a meaningful and purpose-led life. When they talk about their dreams with me, and I see their eyes grow misty, it is my signal to tell them about how I made my dream of living and working overseas come true. I share with them how the universe enjoys playing in the field of possibilities with people who want to leave the world a better place than when they found it. Yes, you can, I affirm. Yes, you must, I exhort. As a mature woman writer and an advocate for women's wisdom, I stand for:

- Perseverance – a gift borne of hardship, challenges, and obstacles that creates the resilience from which our choices and freedom can spring
- The Power of Synchronicities – the language of hope, spoken by the Universe that sparks fruitful connections, inspiration, and dynamic openings into the field of possibilities
- Dreams – the visionary power of inspiration waiting to be choreographed into a dance of real, true life
- Love's Light – the turning point in our heroine's life story in which she take steps toward the dream pounding on the door of her heart, overcomes obstacles, leaves the conventional world for adventures of the soul, and returns triumphant in a creative homecoming that carries a new voice of wisdom, confidence, and strength

May you learn to trust your intuition, for it is one of your premiere mentors. It wants only the best for you—and for the larger world to which you belong. It knows the impact that your inspired actions will have in the grand scheme of things to serve the Greatest Good. It believes in you until you can believe in yourself.

*A life coach and an award-winning author, **Elaine Voci, PhD,** has published eight nonfiction books, and is a member of the International Women's Writing Guild. She has also been named one of the Top Ten Best Life Coaches in Indianapolis by Expertise.com.*

www.elainevoci.com

TRUE WEALTH ISN'T MATERIAL

Sheena Watson

Over the past year I have been in a youth work training program. We had many discussions on the topic of poverty—specifically what life is like for someone who lives below the poverty line. During this time, I was able to serve at multiple soup kitchens and experience the very things we had talked about. My compassion toward those living in poverty has expanded and I now have a completely different perspective. By serving them, sitting with them, and listening to their stories, I was able to see the human hearts behind the faces.

I grew up in an area of Vancouver populated with upper- and middle-class residents. It was easy for me to feel that being surrounded by a high level of wealth was the norm. Just across the water, however, in downtown Vancouver, a large and growing population are living without shelter. My impression growing up was that people who lived on the streets were either criminals or drug addicts; I know now that this isn't always the case.

Poverty can be material, relational, or spiritual. Material poverty is a lack of *things*—basic needs and extra comfort items. Relational poverty is the lack of *people*—family, friends, and people to interact with. Spiritual poverty is the lack of *divine guidance*—specifically from God or other religious affiliations. In all categories, people can be rich or poor at varying levels.

In today's culture, we place a lot of emphasis on what we have; it's the way we display our status or material richness. But it shouldn't be our material wealth that matters—our focus should be on our *relational* and *spiritual* wealth. We were made to be in relationship with one another and experience contentment in life. By having a rich spiritual life and meaningful relationships, we gain a positive sense of well-being and purpose. This is true no matter where you are in terms of material wealth.

One day at the soup kitchen, I had the opportunity to sit with a man and hear his story. He had lived a regular life—he grew up in a middle-class home, went to school, played sports, and had lots of friends. One day at work he injured his back and ended up in the hospital. They gave him morphine for the pain, and after being discharged he had nothing to replace the relief the morphine provided, so he turned to street drugs. One thing led to another, and he found himself unable to work and caught in the cycle of addiction. Now, after some hard work, he is clean and working on getting his life back again. He continues to rekindle his relationship with his family. He shared his passion for God, his motivation to stay clean, and his improving mental health. This man, though not rich materially, was rich in relationships and spirituality. He showed me that not everyone who eats from a soup kitchen is poor—they might even be going there to be able to sit with people and build a community for themselves.

Many people don't have anyone who will take the time to listen to them. No matter how materially rich or poor someone is, anyone can be affected by a relational poverty. *There is power in listening.* By listening to someone, you are empowering them and telling them they are valuable and what they say has value too. You enrich someone relationally by sharing your time with them; you are saying that their time is more valuable to you than the time you could be spending working and increasing your financial richness.

When you see a homeless person, it's easy to think less of them. Little do you know, though, that the person you just walked by could be the most spiritually rich person you have ever encountered. Take the time and sit with someone to hear their story. You might discover that, although you may be on different ends of the spectrum regarding material wealth, they are incredibly rich in other areas of life. The next time you pass someone on the streets, don't be afraid to stop and say hello or ask them about their life. They, like you, have a story—and they may have something to teach you. They may have more wealth and wisdom to share with you than you have to share with them.

Meeting people who live below the poverty line is a very humbling and heartbreaking experience. It has led me to realize that being rich isn't about money—it's about possessing spiritual and relational wealth. We can flourish or languish mentally no matter where we are financially. But when you are rich in relationships and spiritual riches, you will naturally flourish because you will have an increased quality of life emotionally.

No matter who you are, this comes down to what you value. I have learned that being in the right relationship with my family, friends, and God are the things that I value. I know this will allow me to have joy in my life, no matter how many material possessions I have or don't have.

Each person is created with a purpose, and we all have different gifts to share with the people around us. If we keep our gifts to ourselves, other people will miss out; we have gifts so that we can share them, not to make us better than someone else. There is so much value in building relationships with the people around us and getting to know them.

What about you? What do you value? Are you focused on work so you'll be able to treat yourself or your family to material wealth? Do you spend so much time working that there's nothing left over to spend quality time with the people you love? What do you value—and what are you doing to prioritize those values?

Sheena Watson is a university student currently pursuing a teaching degree. She has spent her third year in a specialized program working with marginalized and vulnerable youth. Through this program, she has gained training, experience, and insight into the challenges today's youth face, such as unsupported young families, anxiety, and substance abuse.

www.sheenawatson.com

A SIMPLE STORY OF DEMENTIA, DEVOTION, AND LOVE

Laura Wayman

Why should the world become "dementia-aware"? Across our country and around the world, there is a lack of awareness and understanding of dementia, resulting in stigmatization and barriers to diagnosis and care. This negatively impacts caregivers, families, and societies—physically, psychologically, and economically. The many causes of dementia have increased rapidly into an alarming, silent pandemic. Over half of those seventy years or older will have some form of dementia. The majority of these forms, at this point, have no cure, no prevention, and no way to slow the progressive loss down. Therefore, becoming "dementia-aware" is our best hope to experience positive outcomes as a dementia care provider. As we raise our "dementia-awareness," we learn what dementia is, how it affects the person experiencing dementia symptoms, and particularly how the dementia care journey greatly impacts the family and professional care partners. I teach this essential understanding and totally transformed perception of dementia, which I call becoming "dementia-aware," in order to support, inspire, and encourage the millions of dementia caregivers around the world.

It is possible to simultaneously provide better care both for the person with dementia and the caregiver. However, it becomes necessary to learn and practice a new care approach and changed communication techniques in order to connect and share more meaningful moments with the one being cared for. The complications of confusion, forgetfulness, and memory loss, and the behaviors that go along with them, can be traumatic for the person with the disease and the person providing care. Because of the dementia, neither the individuals involved nor their relationship will ever be the same.

Along with the challenges of caring for a person who has a form of dementia, caregivers—especially family members—will experience conflicting emotions. Their feelings may swing from guilt, denial, and distress one moment to empathy, acceptance, and understanding the next. Not every circumstance is happy, positive, or easy. Caregivers may struggle to find any meaning along the road they are traveling. They may not come to a place of acceptance or understanding about the experience at all.

Below is the moving story of "Peggy," a simple story of dementia, devotion, and love. This poignant true story is an incredible example of a family caregiver who devoted her life to caring for others, her children, foster children, and her beloved husband. I frequently share this story at the beginning of my presentations to illustrate the intensely negative impact dementia care can have on the primary caregiver, especially a same-age spouse, if they do not access appropriate "dementia-aware" support and assistance.

Peggy was a wonderful mother of five, grandmother of fourteen, and wife to her husband, Jack. Over the years, Peggy and Jack had carefully planned for a fun retirement. Their goal was to spend time with the kids and grandkids and travel all over the United States. They had decided years before that they would sell their home at retirement, buy a recreational vehicle, and live the carefree life. And that's what they did, visiting their relatives scattered all over the West and square dancing everywhere they went. After fifteen years in the RV, Peggy sensed that the change to a larger, more stable home was on the horizon. Her large and growing family could not stay with her in the RV, and she needed more space to entertain them.

Jack's health and eyesight had started to decline, and Peggy had to do more of the driving. So Peggy and Jack made the decision to sell their home on wheels. They found a double-wide mobile home in a small town in Northeastern Colorado, which they could afford on their limited budget. It had the disadvantage of being located far away from hospitals, doctors, and senior services, but it was next door to their best friends of forty years. They happily settled in.

Three years passed, and Peggy started to have conversations with her children about Jack's memory loss and other symptoms of dementia. Her daughter offered to help, but Peggy insisted she was OK and would alert her if his condition became unmanageable.

Two weeks after this conversation, disaster struck. When Jack and Peggy sat down to dinner, Peggy suffered a massive heart attack. Jack's reactions to this emergency were slowed by his dementia, which was far more advanced than anyone had realized. By the time the neighbors called 911 and the EMTs arrived, Peggy was already gone.

Peggy's case is a classic example of the devastating effects of caregiver stress. She was not able to paint a precise picture of how much care Jack was receiving (or how much she herself needed). She also was reticent to ask for help, even though family, neighbors, and friends had continually offered to help over the years. She was just doing what she had always done, believing she could do it alone. It ended up taking her life.

If only I could have reached Peggy with "dementia-aware" reinforcement before it was too late—but she was my gentle teacher, showing me that selfless caregivers will take on too much, refusing to ask for or accept help.

And Peggy's story hits home, right into my own heart. You see, Peggy was my mother and my children's grandmother—our very own family hero. This personal experience has driven my passion for educating all caregivers, both family and professional, in the awareness of caring for themselves, along with tips and tools to assist them in effectively caring for memory-challenged adults. My vision is to bring light into the darkness of dementia through support, encouragement, and hope, and to raise "dementia-awareness" worldwide.

My book, *A Loving Approach to Dementia Care*, second edition (third edition coming soon), published by Johns Hopkins University Press—and the specialized education, perceptions, and techniques described within it—will equip all caregivers (professional and family) with the compass needed to navigate this journey to successfully "become dementia-aware."

Laura Wayman, the Dementia Whisperer, *is an internationally renowned author, speaker, and consultant in dementia care. Her methodology is refreshingly different and accessible because of its simplicity and practicality. As a daughter who experienced firsthand the loss of a loved one to dementia, her teachings provide hope by raising "dementia-awareness" worldwide.*

www.laurawayman.com

FREE TO BE

Lisa Wellington

"Look, Mum! A bird!"

I looked where he was pointing, and sure enough there was a little sparrow sitting on the windowsill.

"You know, he's lucky. He has what I don't."

I turned to my little man, laying in his hospital bed, and asked, "What is that?"

"He's free. He can fly wherever he wants to go."

Out of the mouth of babes . . .

My son, Daniel, had figured out a life truth in his six short years on the planet that many adults never figure out.

Life is precious, and the opportunity to make the most of it, on your terms and reflecting your own truth, is a privilege and a gift.

My little boy knew this all too well.

He was diagnosed with leukemia when he was two and had spent most of his life hospitalized or isolated at home. He was the first child in the world diagnosed with brain damage as a result of chemotherapy, and the medical professionals advised us that he would never walk again, swallow properly, or see clearly, and he would have cognitive and motor skill impairment. Their view was that his brain was irrevocably damaged, and there was nothing they could do to change that.

I could not accept this, and so I used my health knowledge I had gained from my own ill-health, my accelerated learning knowledge I acquired from educating leaders in business, and further research into brain nutrients and childhood stages of learning to create a way to bypass the damaged parts of Daniel's brain and create new neural connections.

I did all of this by myself through play designed for a two-year-old confined to a hospital bed or in our family room at home. Twelve months later he was independently assessed by qualified educators on all metrics for his age and deemed to be in the mid-upper percentiles of everything—including socialization.

Brain damage was not the least of his challenges, however; his leukemia returned, requiring a bone marrow transplant and another twelve months of isolation.

At the time of this conversation, we were four years into his journey, and he was back in the hospital after relapsing for the second time. He had glimpsed freedom, thinking that the bone marrow transplant had cured him, and he had started to enjoy having a life which included school and friends. I have a clear memory of him arriving home after a prolonged hospital stay and running around the front lawn trying to fly like a bird, proclaiming, "I'm free! I'm free!"

But this was not to be, and the little bird on the windowsill was a stark reminder. There was no anger or blame in his words—merely a hint of sadness and an acceptance of his situation.

Hearing his comment, my heart broke. Completely. Utterly. Something in the core of my being was touched so deeply that it sparked an immutable fire.

My son fought daily, sometimes even hourly, for the opportunity simply to have another day, in the hope that there would come a time where he had the freedom to determine what he did with it. The unconditional love that opened up in me when he was born ensured that I was with him every step of the way trying to facilitate that opportunity.

When he died, all I wanted to do was curl up into a ball and not come out from under the covers. I was exhausted, sleep-deprived, suffering from post-traumatic stress, and absolutely grieving.

However, I remembered the bird on the windowsill, and I knew the best way to honor Daniel was by being conscious about what I did with my precious moments in every day.

I left my broken marriage and began to build a life as a single non-mother. With all my identities stripped away—wife, mother, caregiver, community participant, school contributor, cancer community participant—I had no idea who I was, or what I was now capable of.

I took a course to learn about computers and the internet, because in the seven years I was totally focused on my son, the internet revolution had started. Initially no one wanted to hire me because I had been out of the workforce for so long. Luckily, I managed to gain a contract in my field of experience—leadership development—and I started to get a renewed sense of myself in the "outside world" and began testing the boundaries of what I could now do.

Powerfully, I discovered that I could no longer go through the machinations of a life that did not align with the core of who I was. I finally had *clarity* on what was important to *me*.

My personal mission became seeing how many lives I could positively touch each day. I gained a coaching qualification, added to my formal qualifications, studied with world-leading neuroscientists to build on my life experience in rewiring my son's brain, and undertook many accredited training programs in a diversity of fields so I could ultimately create unique processes to move myself beyond the consequences of my journey and assist others to create success also.

Aspiring to have the life I envisioned, I moved from the city which had been my home for twenty-two years—leaving behind my friends, some family, and my entire support infrastructure to start anew in a beachside paradise.

While this transformation has been challenging, I'm delighted that ten years later, I now am living all the aspects of my compelling vision: a beachside retreat, a thriving consulting business, health that is getting better and better, extensive travel, and a wonderful man to share my life with.

However, the ultimate gift in my every day is the privilege of partnering with other women to uncover who they truly are and assisting them to successfully create an inspired life and business that makes their heart sing. No judgment. No shame. Just a safe space of grace where they can be Free to BE.

As a futurist, master strategist, and transformational business and life mentor Lisa Wellington brings a unique mix of expansionary insight, performance and energetic knowledge to support evolving women to BEcome conscious leaders in their life and business. Her mission is to enable women to amplify their true essence and soar.

www.lisawellington.com

Spouses Serve Too

Shalanda Tookes Wilder

My cell phone rings, and I hear the tone "Anchors Aweigh" playing. That personalized ringtone means my husband is calling, so I drop what I'm doing to answer the phone. I'm not one to stop what I'm doing whenever my phone rings, but there's some sort of unspoken rule to answer the phone when a military spouse calls.

"I'm up for orders," he says. "Where do you want to move next?"

Those two sentences have been spoken more times than I care to count. Those words mean that it's time for yet another transition. I've always tried to see the bright side of moving every two years or so. As the child of an Army captain, we moved regularly. Now, as the spouse of a Navy officer, we move regularly; however, there is always a bright side. Moving is a chance to leave behind annoying neighbors, pretentious co-workers, and people who turned out to be fair-weather friends. Relocating brings with it the opportunity to meet new neighbors, new business contacts, and new people who may turn into lifelong friends. It's also a chance to experience a different city with a foreign culture. I think everyone should experience a good culture shock at least once in life.

Military transition calls for almost impeccable time management and goal-setting skills, believe it or not. One must coordinate with the household goods office, the movers, current military housing, and military housing at the next duty station. One must also call the medical insurance company, the car insurance company, and let's not forget the schools for those of us who have children. The list goes on, and it's a long one.

Military moves have had a drastic effect on my career goals. A few lucky spouses have not had their careers negatively impacted by the military, but they still have paid a price to keep the momentum going in their careers. Often the price they pay for career focus means they must let their service member move on to his or her next duty station without them. That has not been my story.

My story is one of resiliency and loyalty. I say resiliency because I have suffered many business and career setbacks, but I keep revamping my plan and starting over. I say loyalty because I have supported my husband and his mission with the military despite the upheavals to my life and career. Perhaps you, too, have hit pause on a dream in order to support someone else or focus on something else.

Some people have dared to make comments like "I couldn't follow a man around" or "Your husband needs to start supporting your career because you've supported his career long enough." People who make those ill-informed comments most likely don't understand the military lifestyle and culture.

Those of us who are living this military lifestyle understand that it's necessary to take the good with the bad because we support our spouses as they serve our country. If I were asked to come up with a slogan for military spouses, it would say "Spouses Serve Too." We may not put on a uniform and prepare for war as part of our jobs, but we deal with our own sacrifices and stressors on the home front.

Because I serve too, I relinquished my dream of entrepreneurship. I also dropped my dream of becoming a psychologist. I became frustrated with my lack of time between business building, working toward licensure, raising a family, and spending time with my husband when he was in town.

However, I had to stop using frequent moves and raising a family as an excuse not to pursue my business goals. I can't tell you how many stories I have heard from spouses who allowed their talents and dreams to fade away because they became affiliated with the military.

I started coaching back in 2006, but I gave up due to the stressors of taking care of my family, as well as myself, while running a business full-time. For years I had what I call a nagging feeling inside of me, an urge to restart my coaching business. It bothered me not to use my passion and skill to guide others and it also bothered me when I heard people making excuses as to why they weren't pursuing their dreams and goals. On the other hand, I smile when I get updates from spouses who say they are pursuing a lifelong goal now that their military spouse has retired.

It doesn't have to be this way though. We don't have to hit pause or let the fire within us die because we are supporting a loved one. What would you see if you hit fast-forward? Do you see a person who put their own talents and passions aside to take care of others, or do you envision a resilient, tenacious person who gave their all to build a dream? What will you do with your calling?

I challenge you to reignite that passion inside of you by writing down your list of dreams. Then choose one dream from the list, write down each step needed to reach that dream, and share it with someone. We get a boost of inspiration and motivation by simply verbalizing our dreams. Finally, take one step toward that dream every day, and you will soon find yourself living the life you've always wanted to live.

Shalanda Tookes Wilder is a seasoned career coach and time management specialist with a unique blend of therapy and organizational development. A military brat/military spouse, she understands transitions all too well; therefore, she focuses her work on transitioning military and individuals who want to elevate their careers.

www.tookeswilderguidance.com

Breaking Broadway

Paige Wilhide

Her first love was the stage. Telling someone's story with her voice and body, bringing joy to her audience—it was more than a talent; it was a calling.

By fifth grade, her path to becoming an actress was fast-tracked. She had a talent manager, booked some paid commercial gigs, and was regularly excused from school for rehearsals and auditions. But this dreamer had her sights set on a more ambitious goal, the Holy Grail of the theatre world: Broadway. Each night, as she drifted off to sleep, the dreamer envisioned herself walking down the avenue of sparkling marquees as she sang and danced her way to standing ovations six nights a week.

Finally, at twenty-four years old, she left her home in Baltimore and chased her Broadway dream to New York City.

Upon stepping off the bus, she didn't miss a beat. She immediately got some fresh new headshots and enrolled in acting classes. To pay the bills, she picked up a server job at a nearby restaurant, but just until the big checks from Broadway started rolling in.

It didn't take her long to land her first audition for a role in a small production of *Little Shop of Horrors*. She had painstakingly practiced her audition song "On My Own" from *Les Miserables* until every note was perfect. But that didn't matter during the audition when her nerves boiled to the surface and her throat tightened, forcing her to start two beats too late and a few notes flat.

Halfway through the chorus, the director cut her off. "Thank you. That'll be all."

In that moment the dream deflated like a mylar balloon once so full of life, now shriveled and sinking. For the first time in her life, this dream felt unattainable.

Over the next few months, she continued to hustle, auditioning during the day and working evening shifts at the restaurant. Out of dozens of auditions for independent shows and films, she was cast in a few speaking roles, mostly unpaid and mostly unprofessional.

And then, in October 2012, Hurricane Sandy wreaked havoc on New York City. The restaurant was forced to close. Without warning, her main source of income literally had been washed away. In a fit of desperation, she posted her resume on the Craigslist jobs board with the subject: *Smart, Reliable Personal Assistant Available.* Among the handful of responses was an email from a small accounting firm.

For many twenty-somethings fresh out of college, an interview is a nerve-wracking process that takes weeks of preparation. For this actress, it was just another audition, and if there was one thing she knew, it was how to audition.

"So, tell me about yourself," the founder, Josh, asked with a friendly smile from across the table.

"Well, I'm originally from Baltimore. I moved here to pursue theatre . . ."

"Oh, that's great! A lot of my clients are in the industry."

"Really?" she asked, relieved that she wouldn't have to lie about a passion for helping small accounting firms with their social media.

"Yeah, I know for most people that aren't tax nerds like me, this isn't their first choice of a career."

She nodded knowingly.

"So what kind of ideas do you have for our company?"

She felt those sneaky nerves creeping up again, and her throat began to tighten. This time, she breathed into it and confidently replied, "Well, you definitely need a social media presence, and YouTube is really hot right now. I think creating a series of tax videos would be a great way to stand out."

Josh hesitated for a moment. "Videos? I have such a great face for radio. What about you? Would you be interested in making those videos?"

That question was like a spark, reigniting a fire that had fallen dormant in her. In that instant, her dream was reborn. But it was no longer filled with curtain calls and costumes. That old dream, she realized, relied on other people to call the shots; it would only come to life if the writer created a role that suited her, the agent submitted her, and the casting director liked her. This new dream, the dream to be an entrepreneur, gave her power.

Over the next three years, she built a video production company, trading auditions for weekly networking meetings and acting classes for branding workshops. She transitioned from actress to entrepreneur, using her natural talent for telling stories to help other entrepreneurs tell their stories on camera. Just around the time she felt her home office getting a bit too small for her needs, she heard about a colleague opening a new coworking space downtown.

"Don't mind the mess," Lisa urged, leading her through a maze of scaffolding and construction workers. "We're a little behind schedule."

"I don't mind it at all. I can use my imagination," the dreamer said with a smile.

"Well, here is one of the few two-person offices we still have available," Lisa explained, leading her into a small square marked off with some tape and a metal frame. "As you can see, there is lots of natural light, and if you look out that way, you get a view of . . ."

"The Statue of Liberty!" the dreamer interrupted. It was perfect. "Where do I sign?"

Walking out of the building that day, she thought of the twenty-four-year old that had moved here five years ago—how proud that girl would be of the woman she had become. She had written her own script and cast herself in the director's role, building a life that was everything she had ever wanted.

She swung through the revolving door and stepped onto the sidewalk, corporate suits whizzing by throngs of tourists who had planted themselves to take photos of the building behind her. Turning around to admire the classic arched stone doorway and gold trim of what would become her new office building, she saw it: the address glowing back at her in shiny gold lettering.

26 Broadway.

Paige Wilhide is an actor, director, and video strategist with an obsession for telling stories. She founded Paige Media to help entrepreneurs confidently express themselves in their marketing. Her digital courses and workshops are changing the game for entrepreneurs who want to use video to grow their businesses.

www.paigemedia.com

FIND YOUR SOUL SONG
AND JOIN THE CHORUS

Mary Wong

My heart stopped. With my head spinning, I followed his instructions.
"Don't think they aren't loaded." His voice sounded far away, yet the loaded
guns he showed me were inches from my head.
"If you can't find your shoes, I'll kill you."
I don't want to die, *I screamed in my head over and over.*

At eleven years of age, nobody should fear for their life.

Today I'm a lot of things to a lot of people—wife, mother, friend, confidant, mentor, counselor—but I spent many years feeling used up, worthless, exhausted, empty, and lost.

I grew up the youngest in a family of eight, and I quickly learned that to be heard, I had to be loud.

When I went to school, I continued that pattern, and I became a prime target for schoolyard bullies. But they weren't going to keep me down—I continued to be myself, to speak out, to have a voice.

Until that day at age eleven.

My crime? I had befriended his sister. A year older than us, he was in charge of the house that day while their parents were at work. Hot and tired, I stopped in for a drink of water and left my shoes behind. He hid them behind the piano. When I returned to retrieve them, he met me at the gate and told me if I couldn't find them, he would kill me.

In the aftermath, I was branded a liar and told that I had brought it all upon myself by going into the house. (Stopping anywhere on the way home from school was forbidden.)

My takeaways? *Keep quiet. Don't tell anyone; they won't believe you. Your thoughts are wrong. Your voice has no value.*

From that moment, I squashed my deeper desires and stopped speaking up. I allowed others to tell me what to do, and I conformed to the "good girl" mold. I tried desperately to be perfect, to make sure I never put myself in danger again. With every human slip, I proved myself even more worthless. My life spiraled downward.

I went through several career changes. I was intelligent but seemingly never good enough. Every small error added to my sense of low self-worth. For the most part, I hid my pain behind a smile and people-pleasing. I desperately sought recognition and connection; I longed for someone to tell me I was worth it.

No matter what I did, though, it wasn't enough. I loved my work, but with each career change there was a sense that something was missing; there must be more. I felt like a failure. Why couldn't I complete anything? Why were others so much better than me?

After the birth of my second child, I had a very serious episode of postnatal depression. Recognizing that I was becoming a danger to myself and my children, I sought help.

Therapy—lots of therapy—and personal development helped. Life improved, but something still wasn't right.

Then, out of the blue, came a strong reminder of those guns at the gate . . .

A routine blood test revealed a diagnosis of leukemia. This time, the words echoing in my head were *I want to live!* It was as if someone flipped a switch in my inner being.

Drawing on my counseling training, I employed positive psychology, reframing the negatives and making space for positive energy at every turn. As I meditated, focusing on healing, I found an unexpected benefit. In the peaceful space of meditation, my inner voice emerged. I learned to listen to myself, and I became my own best friend. Instead of judging myself harshly when I displayed imperfection, I spoke with the hurt child within, guiding and mentoring myself, and that is where the biggest magic began.

I allowed myself to speak out about my inner desires, and a whole new world opened itself up to me. Prior to the diagnosis, I had been successfully speaking and training internationally with a nonprofit organization for several years. While I was doing well in the field, I was aware that my speaking lacked something special. I had the skills, and I could deliver a message in a manner that connected with my audience, but it was automatic, coming from my head.

Speaking my truth from the heart was a whole new learning curve. I had to learn to allow others to see the real me—the girl that had been ridiculed and excluded as a child. That took an enormous leap of faith!

I started by speaking my truth to smaller audiences—one or two people at most. Then gradually I spoke to larger groups. I focused on building my training and speaking business. I started by running a networking group—a space where I was able to stretch my comfort zone and practice speaking authentically. I met phenomenal and inspiring people who had brilliant ideas for making a huge difference in the world. They needed to learn to speak and lead their cause to create their legacy. Working with them, I realized that I had found the space where I truly belonged. The emptiness was gone.

I always felt I had a legacy to leave, but I didn't know what it was. Now I realize that my legacy is empowering others to leave *their* legacy. I now help others realize their greatness, the power of their personal story, and the ability to speak out and engage a following to create change for good.

It's truly beautiful to finally feel like I belong, to finally know that I have worth and my work is valuable. The more I speak my truth, the more magic appears. I have found my path, and my soul is singing!

The leukemia has been in treatment-free remission for over twelve months now. I truly believe that living my soul-purpose is what allowed that to happen.

If you are holding back from speaking out, I encourage you to make the necessary changes and let your soul join the chorus. The music here is divine!

Mary Wong is an author, speaker, mentor, and the founder of Optimal Life Solutions. An experienced coach, counselor, and corporate trainer, she assists her clients to bring their hidden voices to light so they can speak out, step up, and create a legacy of lasting change that will positively impact the world.

www.optimalcoaching.com.au

Step Out of the Shadow
and into Your Light

Kamini Wood

"I was always looking outside myself for strength and confidence. But it comes from within. It was there all the time." —Anna Freud

Codependency takes different forms. You can be codependent on another person, on pleasing other people, or on external validations, or some combination of these. This codependency on pleasing others makes us vulnerable to toxic relationships. That was my experience.

I grew up in a small town in Connecticut. My family was one of only a couple Indian households in a predominantly white town. There was a constant underlying feeling of wanting to fit in, wanting to be accepted. Therefore, imprinted early on was the need to please others, to take care of them in an effort to be accepted. Over time this morphed into a dependency of external validation. All my validation of "being a good person" came directly from measuring if others were happy around me and whether I did enough to make them happy. I carried this with me through my teenage years and into adulthood.

Becoming a mother and raising my children finally became the catalyst for change. I learned to become an observer of my behaviors and stepped into a place of empowerment. My journey caused me to question how I could create a balance between caring for others and being your own self-leader.

I discovered that the pathway from codependent to independent self-leader comes from being an observer, allowing space for emotions, learning nonjudgment, and performing self-compassion. These four pillars lead a woman into her own being, where she can confidently make decisions and manage the pressures of life. She will learn that she is not meant to be "everything to everyone," but instead, she is meant to be her authentic self. By doing this, she shows up, is present, and can give genuine love to others.

Observing I needed others to be happy first. If they needed or more importantly wanted something, there I was to make sure I helped them achieve it. That is where my self-worth came from. I ended up being a task master, jumping from one item on my to-do list to the next. I was literally a pawn in my own life, being played by others.

After years of living to please others, I stepped back and observed the actions of others, how they treated me, how they spoke to me. I observed their expectations of me and how I responded. I finally saw how I had allowed my life to be overrun by others. My thoughts, actions, desires were dictated by others.

Emotional Awareness and Release Codependency on external validation meant suppressing my own emotions. As my oldest daughter entered her teenage years, I had the biggest wake-up call. I saw her suppressing her feelings.

We learn to suppress our emotions through various techniques we learn through culture and society, such as being distracted, numbing our feelings through overeating or drinking too much, smiling on the outside but feeling awful on the inside, or even turning to affirmations and attempting to convince ourselves we don't actually feel a certain way by filling ourselves with "positive thoughts." While these techniques have the appearance of working, our emotions are still swirling around subconsciously and will find a way to reappear until we finally notice them. Our reality gets distorted when we don't allow ourselves to feel our emotions.

We need to recognize that in vulnerability there is power and strength. Giving emotions a place to exist and just be opens up a whole world of possibility.

Nonjudgment At dinner one evening, my five-year-old, who is extremely type A, had an absolute meltdown. During the course of carrying her plate from the counter to the table, the sauce on her plate had mixed with the peas. She does not like her foods to be mixed, and this made her very angry. And she let it be known quite vocally. I chose to let her do her thing and quietly kept eating my meal. My other four children were losing their cool. "Make her stop, Mom!" "This is so annoying." Previously I would have tried to fix things and end the tantrum. But I had learned to honor and *not judge*. I let it go; I let her do her thing. After three minutes, she was eating and laughing and teasing her ten-year-old brother.

The lesson: My five-year-old allowed her anger to be, without judgment or attachment. It rose, it crested, it receded. And she was able to see clearly that all was fine with world and move on. I too practiced nonjudgment. I didn't try to stop the emotion or fix the situation. Above all, I did not judge the anger. I just let it be what it was.

We as women can learn to allow our emotions to be what they are and acknowledge them: "I see you [anger, sadness, fear, stress]." If we let ourselves live through the "wave" and then simply move forward without being critical, we are well on our way to self-leadership.

Self-Compassion Self-esteem is very important. It is the idea that we believe in ourselves and think positively about ourselves. Self-confidence is also equally important. It is the belief in ourselves that we can accomplish anything we set our mind to. However, there is a third piece, and that is self-compassion. This is the acceptance of self. It's forgiving ourselves for shortcomings or personal failings. It's allowing space to be who we are. It's learning to say, "I'm OK." The more you open yourself to be compassionate with yourself, the more you learn to be compassionate with others—but it will be from a place of independence rather than dependence.

These four pillars empower us to step out from the shadow and into our light. Becoming an independent self-leader is all about becoming an observer and developing emotional honesty, nonjudgment, and self-compassion. When we live these truths, we become a powerful voice of the 21st century.

Kamini Wood is a certified life, wellness, and teen life coach. She also is board-certified through the AADP. She works with teen girls and women of all ages, leading them on their own journey toward inner confidence, authenticity, and self-leadership so they can become leaders in personal and business matters.

www.itsauthenticme.com

We'd like to introduce *The Silver Lining of Cancer*

This collection of inspirational stories from thirteen courageous women was created in an effort to positively impact the lives of people who have been diagnosed with cancer and their families.

Our mission is to deliver *The Silver Lining of Cancer* into the hands of people across the world who need some inspiration, hope . . . and a guide to look for the silver lining at a scary time in their lives.

If you want to help us with our mission, we invite you to purchase a copy and share it with your family and friends, or purchase one as a gift for someone going through trying times.

We also invite you to purchase and donate books that will be delivered to support centers around the world.

Do you or someone you know want to be part of our next book?

We'd love to hear from you!
Please join us on our Facebook Page
http://bit.ly/silverliningfb

More details can be found on our Facebook page or on our website at
https://thesilverliningofcancer.com

"I alone cannot change the world, but I can cast a stone across the waters to create many ripples."
MOTHER TERESA

It's Time for Your Voice to Be Heard!

As women step up as leaders in every industry, on every continent, Women Speakers Association is here to support you to feel empowered to speak from any stage, whether it be directing a boardroom, hosting a webinar, leading a session at the UN, etc.; to use your voice to guide, inspire, educate, train, and motivate.

With over thirty years' experience behind the scenes in the speaking industry, we know how challenging it can be to position yourself powerfully as a woman in order to get your message out and make the difference you came here to make.

We're Here to Help Grow Your Visibility So You Get Seen, Booked, and Paid!

We are here to provide solutions to the issues you tell us are most important to you, whether that's getting booked on the big stages, growing your visibility, promoting your events and products, or bringing you a sense of community when you feel like you're out there going it alone.

Be Part of the First-Ever Global Gathering Place for Women Speakers in Over 120 Countries

We invite you to join us in this collaborative, conscious "movement," a growing sisterhood reaching women in 120 countries on six continents transforming how you get yourself and your message out into the world. We're here to help you positively impact the lives of your clients, your companies, your communities, and the world.

 WOMEN SPEAKERS ASSOCIATION

www.WomenSpeakersAssociation.com

CPSIA information can be obtained
at www.ICGtesting.com
Printed in the USA
BVHW041201250919
559149BV00057B/984/P